SERVE

My Lost Years at the Heart of Ireland's Opus Dei

ANNE MARIE ALLEN

GILL BOOKS

Gill Books
Hume Avenue
Park West
Dublin 12
www.gillbooks.ie

Gill Books is an imprint of M.H. Gill and Co.

9781804582862

Designed by Padraig McCormack
Edited by Liosa McNamara
Copy edited by Esther Ní Dhonnacha
Proofread by Tamsin Shelton
Printed and bound in Great Britain by Clays Ltd, Elcograf S.p.A.
This book is typeset in 11pt on 17.5pt, Sabon LT Pro

*The paper used in this book comes from the wood pulp
of sustainably managed forests.*

This book is a memoir and work of creative non-fiction. It reflects the author's recollections of experiences over a specific number of years and the author's interpretation of conversations that took place during that period. To protect the privacy of individuals, some names, events and identifiable characteristics have been changed, compressed or recreated for literary effect.

*To the best of our knowledge, this book complies in full with
the requirements of the General Product Safety Regulation (GPSR).
For further information and help with any safety queries,
please contact us at productsafety@gill.ie.*

A CIP catalogue record for this book is available from the British Library.

5 4 3 2 1

I dedicate this to all survivors of domestic servitude imposed on them by Opus Dei.

'I tell my story not because it is unique, but because it is not. It is the story of many girls.'

Malala Yousafzai

Prologue

There is a house not far from Tuam in Galway. One of those gorgeous Georgian estate houses with grounds, built centuries ago, that no doubt held lavish parties and banquets and kept people for miles around in employment. Houses like that, they're part of Irish history. This one is part of my history.

Ballyglunin Park and I know each other well, because it was taken from the life it had and turned into something destructive, stripped of its adornments and its nature and made use of, like I was. It was used to do wrong, and I was too, inside of the walls where I was kept. Even now, 40 years later, that house and I are the same. Something reconstructed but not recovered.

Who would I be if I had never gone there? I think I would like to meet the woman I was becoming, before Opus Dei pulled me in with their fearmongering and their spiderwebs. Would I be a better person, or a lesser person? Or maybe someone wilder and freer, totally different?

All I know is maybe that woman would be good. It was what I wanted for myself, before all of this: to be a good person. But I don't know if I ever had that figured out at all. What is good? I still don't know.

Maybe I am who I was meant to be. I hope so. I've had to fight hard for absolutely every single thing I have now, and I still don't feel like a whole person. I feel like half. Or less. I have these empty spaces, pockets inside of my ideas, and I still don't know where I'm going. I've done my best. It's all I could do. I left Opus Dei with the clothes on my back and years of neglect, coercion, fear and brainwashing to recover from – as much as I could. You don't really recover fully from it.

The woman I was becoming is lost. I know it. Maybe she is left behind in the walls of Ballyglunin Park, with the hopes and dreams she arrived there with. I miss her, wherever she is, though I have no way to know her. She runs like a shadow through my mind, a glimpse of a life without the shame they forced into my persona.

We don't get to go back. We only get to walk forward in this life, one way through, and I suppose that's the hardest thing about it. I was a child born into the prison of my gender, caged by my culture, and in Ireland back then we had it hard enough – blamed for the moves made on us, blamed for things men did. But I had no youth, no crazy heady summers full of that glorious expression of girlhoods all over the world, even in such a restrictive place as Ireland was then. I never danced with a boy, or cut my hair when he broke my heart. At the age when most girls are figuring things out, I was making vows of celibacy to a god I didn't understand. When most girls my age were falling in love, I was a slave.

The memory is hard to bear.

I want to talk it through, tell you about it. It's important. I want to tell you all about those people, the ones caught up too, the ones pulling the strings. The ones who took everything from me in the name of something foolish, something human.

God. Does He even exist? You know, He probably does. Does He care what I gave up for Him? I doubt it. I doubt all of it, and I have pushed my fist into His bleeding side more times than I should.

God.

The reality of what the fear of Him did to me takes me over sometimes, drowns me.

Oh, to put my arms around her and tell her, 'Don't go, Anne Marie, it will all work out.'

If only I could.

Ballyglunin Park has been rescued from those people, and I have been rescued from those people. We were both set free to come back to the land of the living, where parties and people are, where we eat and drink and laugh, where we mourn the dead and drink and cry and talk for hours and where we disagree and fight and lose the head. This world, where we give ourselves up to living a life, because we only have one. We only have one, don't we?

And we deserve to be what we were built for.

One

Our kitchen at home was cold. Mam worked all the time. Dad said once that it was because she didn't want to think. Maybe that was true. My mother's thoughts were the kind that could bring a person to the brink.

So in 1978, at 15, when I wasn't in school, I was doing all the things a mother would normally do, because mine was working double shifts: the cooking and the cleaning and the running of a home – that was left to me. I was pretty upset about it too; coming into my own mind as a teenager gave me a sense of unfairness that grumbled out of me as I washed up the bowls my brothers had left around, with spoons still in the congealing milk from old breakfasts. I cooked their dinners, all the usual Irish dinners, stews and mince on spuds, all of that. I did their laundry and made their beds. I cleaned the house and hated them for it, because they were born boys so they didn't have to lift a finger. If my mother *was* home, and we were all there, it would still be my name called to do whatever it was, even though I had done everything else every day that she wasn't. I was responsible for getting my brothers to school, and to Mass on Sundays, pulled up if I didn't manage it, the responsibility of them all mine even though they should have been well able.

So by the time I was old enough to go looking for a part-time job I could cook the dinners blindfolded. And so it fell in that I would be taken on at the local hotel, the Grand, where Mr and Mrs Murphy ran a tight ship.

The hotel sits on the main road in Ballyvourney, County Cork, where we were living. We'd come home from England a few years before all of this, on account of Mam being Mam. Maybe Dad wondered if Ireland, and the things she was more used to from her old life, could help. But they didn't. Mam didn't really notice the world around her anyway.

'Sure don't you want to be a chef?' the family would all say when I complained. I did want to be a chef, but I knew I wasn't going to get to be one in my own home, pouring hot water into Smash powder or reheating cold chicken and ham that Mrs Murphy had given me to take home after a chicken supper cancelled one weekend.

'Waste not want not,' she had said.

In the Grand, Mr Murphy, the owner, did all the cooking, standing over his cooker and looking over his glasses through the steam and smoke and spitting oil of whatever was ordered, the trays and trays of roast chicken in the oven, plated with stuffing that we mixed in a huge baby bath and served with vegetables that came out of the warmer. He used our second names, not our first – like soldiers in a platoon.

Mr Murphy made sauces and soups and stews and at dinnertime, after the guests had been served, he would pull up a chair with all of us and we would all be fed while he read the paper, and he would talk to us in bits and bobs about the events we might have that week. 'Two hundred people for a dinner dance on Saturday night, no bother to ye.'

Groans and gasps all around, knowing we would be run off our feet with it.

'If there's to be chaos,' he would say, looking over his glasses at us while turning the page on his newspaper, 'let it be organised chaos ...'

Mr Murphy always said that line and we always hummed and hawed in response, making promises to him that we would keep our heads. The kitchen, when he was in it, ran like clockwork. But it was outside, where we were serving, that sometimes got away from me. When it did, Mrs Murphy would catch me by the elbow and make me stand for the count of 10, reminding me that in her hotel, everyone *would* get fed and everyone *would* be happy.

'Serve *one* person at a time,' she would tell me. 'Calm yourself, keep the head.'

It was good advice for an overwhelmed teenager, but I was never a fan of serving. Instead I vied for the spot beside Mr Murphy, on the pass, dishing out Sunday dinners one after the other. He would slice the turkey meat perfectly in thin, identical slices, and send them to his right, for me to put a tablespoon of stuffing on and send the plate right again to Declan Murphy, the eldest son, who would ladle a lash of gravy over that dinner so perfectly he never so much as spilled a drop.

Mr Murphy looked for me sometimes to take that place beside him, and when he did it filled me with a confidence I got nowhere else. Each time he looked for me by name, I swear I grew an inch taller. Because of those boosts, I took pride in my work, a pride that followed me up through the hotel, where I would make perfect beds and leave bathrooms sparkling. In school, at home, nobody gave me praise at all, and I believe that all children need it. Outside the Grand I felt like I was nothing much, but inside of that hotel I was 'Allen', Mr Murphy's right-hand woman, as he would say.

'*Íosa Chríost!*' Mr Murphy would curse in Irish, any time he turned around for something that wasn't there, neglected by his team of teenage girls who would get sidetracked by rumours of a good-looking boy in the dining room. Weren't we girls in a tiny village in the middle of the countryside? Those coach groups brought with them dreams of love and romance, the kind that we only ever saw on the television, which we talked about all the time.

'Did you see *Napoleon in Love* last night?' someone would say, and we would be away with our imaginations, weak at the knees with what could be ahead of us once we found the One. My dad would never have allowed me watch shows like that, but sure wasn't he always out? I watched all the television shows, and so I could always join in swooning over Ian Holm as Napoleon, or Patrick Duffy as Bobby Ewing in *Dallas*.

'The fellas around here are brutal,' Carrie Power used to say, and we would all agree. Then word would go around that there was a coachload of GAA players pulling into the car park and we would all drop whatever task we were halfway through to get a look.

Carrie Power was older than me, one of four older girls, all 17 and 18 – her, Angela Mullen, Tara Ford and Leanne Trudo, whose father was the garda. I knew them from Mass, not school. They always sat at the back, and they always talked. I never had the courage to talk at Mass, but I wished I did. I used to imagine as I walked in that one of them would pull me to sit beside them and whisper to me too, like they did to each other. But that never happened.

Those four always made plans to go into the nearby town, Macroom, to buy clothes on pay day, or to do something in the church, and they always asked me to cover for them, or finish their rooms or jobs, and I would never say no and then I would be late myself, and in trouble at home again.

But, thankfully, also working in the Grand was Niamh Moore, who I met on day one and clicked with instantly, even though I was 15 and she was 13.

'And a half,' Niamh would say. She didn't look 13: she was taller than all of us, with huge brown eyes and black curly hair that flew everywhere and a husky laugh that would take her totally over, and then me too, in that way contagious laughs do, where you find yourself doubling over and breathless even though you don't know what you're laughing at. She was always making me laugh – most of the time not on purpose.

One day in particular she had in her hands a tray of individual trifles, in those little metal dishes with stems, and they had started to slide off one side, so she counterbalanced and lost two off the other side straight onto the floor. She gave a small screech when she realised. The containers bounced off the lino, leaving their contents in two blobs at her feet. She staggered for a minute, trying to control the tray, the trifles sliding over one side and then the other.

'Lord bless us and save us, Moore, will you put that tray down?!' Mr Murphy said, and so she did, placing it back onto the counter while pressing her lips together as hard as she could and avoiding all eye contact with me.

'Don't move,' I said, and hunkered down with a cloth, using one bowl to push the trifle into another, intending to lift them into the bin. But Niamh stepped back, putting a heel into the part I was pushing forward, and I squealed and could not stop laughing.

'Oh Jesus,' Niamh said, lifting her foot backward to see. I wiped the heel of her shoe and the floor, and she hunkered down and helped, and we got it cleaned up.

We realised then that Mr Murphy was glaring over the top of his glasses at us, because we were distracted by each other and hadn't heard what he had just asked us to do.

We stared back at him.

'Bins,' he repeated, and Niamh and I then went for the same bag, sending each other into absolute hysterics again. 'For the love of —' Mr Murphy was about to lose it, so we stifled our giggles, and I grabbed the bag and handed it to Niamh, and she left the kitchen with it.

As she left and the door swung, I heard Tara Ford say, 'Carrie says there is a fine thing down in the bar,' and so I followed Niamh out and she abandoned the bin bag there and we ran down to the bar, skidding to a stop at the door before we went through it, and then, full of nonchalance, we sauntered in and across the room to the other side, looking like we had business there, turned and walked nonchalantly out again, getting as good a look as we could at the guy in question – all big hair and bell-bottoms – clutching at each other's sleeves and jumpers as we did.

'I'd die for a lad like that,' Niamh said as soon we were back in the hall, and she flattened herself against the wall, swooning as Tara and Carrie came toward us. They always wore the latest thing. I had no sisters, and these girls were so grown-up and cool. I wanted their attention, but I rarely got it. So when I did, I thrived.

'Did you see him?' Tara asked.

We nodded.

'He is a fine bit of stuff,' she declared.

'I bet he is from Cork City,' I said.

'They're American tourists,' Carrie said, in the know.

'He looks like David Cassidy,' I said.

'I shifted a guy who looked like him before, from Enniskeane,' Carrie said, and I was in awe of her.

'I love David Cassidy,' I said straight to her with a smile.

But she wrinkled up her nose. 'Bit goody-goody for me.'

I felt a sting. 'Yeah, I don't like him either,' I said, dying inside as soon as I heard myself. The older girls looked at each other as if to say, 'What is this one on?' and so I turned and walked away, mortified and telling myself I was stupid the whole way back to the kitchen.

Mr Murphy gave me a long, hard look when I came back in. 'I was looking for you,' he said, and pulled his knife expertly back and forth on an onion, spreading it out then in thin slices.

'Sorry, Mr Murphy.'

'There's 15 orders come in for soup and sandwiches.' He nodded toward the platters that were stacked high in the corner. 'And those plates are absolutely manky.'

I went to work straight away, and he huffed and puffed for a minute, chopping the salad, and then he said, 'Have you plans after the Inter Cert, Anne Marie?'

'Getting the hell outta here, I hope.' I said it without thinking, and then I felt bad, because I loved Mr Murphy and everyone else in Ballyvourney, outside of my house. What I wanted from life I had no idea really. I knew that I was good in the kitchen: even if Mr Murphy never told me, I could feel that I was doing the right thing. Everywhere else I went I was never sure of that at all.

'Ah.' Mr Murphy seemed like he had heard this before. He stopped chopping and looked at me with a sigh. 'Dublin, is it?'

'No way, Mr Murphy,' I said, wanting to slip back into his good graces. 'I'm going to London.'

'London?' he said sceptically, and went back to chopping. 'Sure what's in London?'

'I was born over there,' I said, and he nodded slowly as if mulling over the idea, 'and I'm going to go back there ...' I said as if it wasn't just a plan I'd thought up right that moment, 'to train in cooking. I want to be a chef,' I pointed at his chopping board, 'like you!' I ended cheerfully.

'Ah, you do, do you?' he said, sliding the chopped veg into a bowl and taking another onion. 'Well, come back to me when you get your cert-if-i-cate,' his Cork accent dancing over the word, 'and I'll give you a good job.'

I was charmed with that. 'You will?'

'You're the best girl we have here,' he said, and pointed his knife at me.

I was so filled up with pride it burst out of me in a smile that made him smile back at me briefly, before he turned back to his work with a cough and a shake of his head.

'There will always be a job here for you, anyway,' he said.

'Thanks, Mr Murphy,' I said, and I stood looking at him for a minute, before he said, 'Plates!' loud enough to send me scuttling back to work. I washed those plates like I was in the all-Ireland finals of plate-washing, I swear I did.

Two

My mother had two sisters. Eileen was a married woman living behind just up the way, and Bernadette was a nun who lived in England. Most Irish families had nuns and priests in them. It was nothing unusual. I loved my aunts fiercely, Eileen because she made me flower girl at her wedding and Bernadette because she used to take me on holidays.

There was an old house in Scarborough that once a year would be vacated by the nuns who lived there, for whatever reason, perhaps a pilgrimage, and Bernadette and I would sleep in their little rooms surrounded by their small things, and I loved every minute of it. We would drive from Portsmouth, singing songs and telling stories on the long journey. Once or twice one of my brothers might be brought as well, sometimes my mam, but mostly it was only me.

On those holidays Bernadette would organise our days on a list that she would keep in the flat front pocket of her black handbag, and strike each event through with a blue biro as we completed it, the sheet of paper pressed against her hand. I relished the routine, being woken and washed and fed with a good breakfast, and then dressed and brushed and teeth done and coat on and out the door to wherever we were going.

On picnics she would gently spread a small white napkin out on the grass between us, and fuss in her bag, taking out a little packet with perfectly cut sandwiches that she laid down on the napkin, and then a bag of cut apples, and a flask of tea. 'We will have to share that cup, now,' she would tell me. I didn't mind; I would have drunk from her hand, I loved my Auntie Bernadette so much.

At dinner time she would make potatoes and vegetables and serve them hot with gravy and butter and some salt that she would sprinkle from pincered fingers across my plate.

In the convent there was all kinds of old furniture and old books, and huge fireplaces, and a long clock on the wall that ticked and hummed on the hour because the chimes were gone on it. In the evenings, we would sit in the drawing room and Bernadette would light a fire, because of course even in summer it would get cold in an old house, keeping me in my coat until she got it going. She would break small sticks that we had gathered in the grounds, and I loved the way her knuckles would flex, and her fingers would press away until the twigs snapped. We would have rolled and tied paper into pretzels as firelighters the night before – we did that before we went to bed, about ten each would do – and so she would take those and light them and force them in among the sticks, and before long a good fire would be taking and the room would warm up.

On some evenings Bernadette would read, and the room would be so quiet except for the sound of her page turning. I would draw or write, play around with the tassels of the huge velvet curtains around the windows for a while, or find some object to make a character out of. Sometimes she would knit for a while or teach me to knit, and the room would fill up with the warmth and so would I, on the inside, wishing that I could live forever with Bernadette. I loved the sound of her knitting needles.

Around the edges of the ceiling were friezes of people and animals and around the light, too, in the middle. Other times if I was playing and I got sleepy, I would roll onto my back and lie there on the warm floor in the quiet, when Bernadette would go through the records there, one by one, and I would listen to the sound that made as she pulled the sleeves away and let them drop. Those evenings she would play hymns and beautiful instrumentals on the record player, and I would fall asleep listening.

I loved the soft voice she used when she called my name and gave me a little caress on my cheek, telling me it was time to go on to bed because I was falling asleep. She would lift me into an old creaky iron cot that had been put in her room for the week.

'I don't want to go to bed,' I would tell her, because the room was cold and the bed was like ice.

'We sometimes have to do things we don't want to do,' Bernadette would tell me, impressing it into me with a soft hand to my cheek, 'but when we want to be good, we *do* the things that are uncomfortable and we do them for *God*. That is what makes us good, and that is what helps us fight against the Devil.'

I was afraid of the Devil. I'd seen pictures of him in the Bible in school. I never wanted to fight him, with his horns and hooves. I wanted to stay as far away from him as I could.

Bernadette would stroke my hair and pray with me, in words I didn't know the meaning of and with intention I didn't have. As I got older we would both pray on our knees together, rhythmical calming chants that went on and on, repeating, and where we would take turns to say one bit and have the other answer.

Those rhythms took over you, and your mouth would go without even thinking.

We used to say the Hail Mary over and over, and Bernadette would look at my eyes and I would look at hers, and it felt so warm and safe. That was really normal for Catholics on both sides of the Irish Sea, in the seventies. Everyone prayed before they went to bed, and the prayers were full of fear and Hell and not dying in your sleep. I really wanted to be good.

It was so peaceful. If I'd known how to express myself at that age *peace* would have been the word I'd have used. Home was chaotic, with a mother there in body but not in mind, and rambunctious brothers. When I was older there was a trundle bed on the floor where I would sleep, out for the count, in total peace with the window open full of sea air, and no fear of being woken by a rowdy pair of brothers in my room, or by my mam's voice calling because she needed the curtains closed or because I had to run an errand.

When Bernadette would wake me the next morning, I'd eat a plate of hot sausages and eggs and warm toast with melted butter and we would go again.

'You've always been great company, Anne Marie,' my aunt Bernadette told me.

―――――

My aunt Bernadette had it all together as much as my parents did not. Her life was orderly and filled with quiet, while our house was hectic and full of chaos, with brothers who got away with murder, who would tease you and mortify you and never got in trouble for it or anything else.

Whereas I got in trouble for everything.

The rest of them could be lying around all day, and I would come inside and get told off something shocking for leaving *their* breakfast bowls unwashed, and I would have to do it there and then. And so it felt to me like I was always in trouble – always being chastised for something. So I complained a lot and I sulked a lot, let me tell you. It was easy to point fingers because I knew who to point them at: my brothers, whose lives seemed so easy, in from school and straight back out again to GAA or bike around or go wherever they wanted, or just to lie on the floor or the sofa watching TV, whereas I got questioned and asked who I was with and what I was doing for every second, always given tasks and housework. Always warned non-stop about terrible things.

You see, the influence of the Church in Ireland was through everything.

There was a complete and total normalisation of religion, not like today. If a teenager was asked today what they were doing at the weekend and they said they were heading to do the Stations of the Cross, or Benediction, they would get worried looks, I am sure of it. But back then, that *was* a totally normal teenage activity.

I was always getting caught watching the telly and scolded. It was *Dynasty* or *Dallas*, or some romantic TV series that the whole world seemed to be watching.

'I am tired of telling you, Anne Marie,' my dad would say, 'this show is not suitable for a young woman, do you hear me?'

I'd try to *plámás* him, I'd tell him everyone was watching it. But there were two subjects my father liked to worry about. TV was the first worry.

'You stay away from boys,' he said all the time, about the other one. 'Do you hear me, Anne Marie?'

He was always making sure I knew to stay away from boys. I will be honest with you: I was so innocent then, I didn't really know what he meant, since the man himself had enrolled me in a school full of them. My brothers and I went to the boarding school in Ballyvourney, as day students, because it was nearby.

'*An bhfuil Gaeilge aici?*' a Christian Brother had asked my father at my interview. *Does she speak Irish?*

'*Tá, tá,*' Yes, yes, my father had replied, patting me on the head and pushing me forward as the ideal candidate, because the only school in walking distance was this one and my parents hated an extra bill. They were bad enough with money, and rooting around in the morning for children's bus fare to go to school was a hassle they wanted to avoid.

'I don't think they're teaching you properly in that school,' my mother said once, but sure they could have been – I wouldn't have known about it. I hadn't a word. I barely understood a word said to me at school, but nobody ever noticed.

I was left out and left behind a little because of that. Some girls used to smirk at my clothes, because we had no uniform and I only had a couple of bits of fashion that I had managed to get with my wages from the hotel. I had a little sleeveless jumper and a pair of jeans, but my shoes were old and worn out and from the last fashion trend. I used to dream about the clothes I could wear if I didn't have parents that couldn't see the point in new clothes when I had some in the wardrobe, or new shoes when I had a perfectly good pair on my feet. I used to try to wear them out on my way home, scuffing them up, but Dad would tell me to polish them and say they would do me for another while.

'Nice shoes,' the mean girl would say when I wore them into school. There were comments like that from her almost every day. She picked on me and I had no idea why. Now I know why: because boys always chatted to me in class. I just had no idea I was pretty. But I was, really.

So when Dad had a go at me, warning me to stay away from boys, I just shrugged and agreed even though he was asking the impossible. I could hardly actually ignore my classmates. The boys always spoke to me, asking for a lend of a pencil or to copy my homework. I'd tried to ignore them, sometimes. But some of them would badger me and I could never hold out.

At Mass, the priest was always saying it as well, that what went on between men and women was sinful. ''Tis a mortal sin,' he would say soberly, and wag his finger, telling us to go to Confession. In school one of the Brothers would talk about Hell and how to get there.

'Lust!' the monk would cry out about the Devil incarnate, but never actually explain what that was. 'Being lustful is a sin. Sins send you to Hell.'

My mam, rarely, would broach the subject as well: 'Just stay away from those boarders, do you hear me?'

I agreed and promised. But of course, I couldn't keep that promise either. The boarders, from all over Ireland, were funny and friendly and I had to talk to them – of course I did. They were in my class.

'You know what happens to girls,' Mam would tell me.

'Do they get killed?' I asked her, not sure.

'Worse,' she said. 'Worse than that.'

I had no idea what was worse than being killed. Some terrible thing.

'You'll go straight to Hell,' I was warned over and over, by every adult I knew, 'if you commit mortal sins with boys.'

I knew exactly what Hell was. I had been told. It was a huge pit under the earth, full of fire and molten lava – where the Devil lived. The smell and pain of fire were something I knew: one Christmas when I was barely five, my mother sent our letters up to Santa in the fire. I leaned a little bit too far in and set fire to my own hair.

Then, not long after that accident, an old uncle of my father's, who lived back along, got very cranky with me for knitting on a Sunday when he visited our house.

'You will go straight to Hell for that,' he told me, pointing at my pink knitting needles and blue yarn, 'a mortal sin – you'll burn in the fire forever for the likes of that.'

I put them on the windowsill and never dared take up those needles again.

———

By the time I was a teenager I had learned a few lessons on how to stay out of Hell. But some things were too hard to resist. And sure, despite the prayers and the promises and all the warnings, humans are still human and by the time I got to the end of my fifteenth year, I had myself a favourite boy.

Dan Gallagher was a West Cork lad who looked like every hero I had watched on TV, tall and tanned with a mop of brown curly hair that fell into his eyes. I'd seen him leaning on the far wall at the céilí a couple of times, looking at me. I'd looked away.

Being lustful is a sin. Sins send you to Hell.

In school we had a movie day at the end of the year, and toward the end of it Dan made his way to me in the gym hall, where they'd pulled down the blinds and filled the floor with us all sitting in rows, and he whispered to me to meet him at the back of the school after. I knew why. Everyone went around there to kiss.

'You have to go,' one of the girls told me. 'He asked you.'

I was faced with a terrible choice. Hell, or whatever would happen if I didn't go to kiss Dan. Hell was farther off, so I went with that. I could say a lot of rosaries, I told myself.

And so, even with the sound of my mother's warnings beating in my ears, I went and let Dan kiss me, and instantly I felt terrible, real shame deep inside. When he walked me around the front again, some of the other boys from our class made whooping sounds so I ran away.

Down the road, away from them, I blessed myself, but it only made me feel worse. When I got home I took the Bible upstairs and read it, even though I didn't understand most of what I was reading. I was sure that would compensate for the sins I had committed. It was also a sin to dishonour your parents, so I was in for a double whammy.

'We rang Auntie Bernadette from the village phone box earlier,' my mam told me. 'She said she was sorry you were not there.'

I was glad I'd missed her. Bernadette was so *good* and clearly I was bad to the bone. I spent the days after that worrying about God and Hell and making my mother sicker than she already was.

'Your mother finds things a bit hard,' my aunt Bernadette said to me one time when we were away, and she whispered a little prayer and blessed herself and looked up to Heaven for ages with her mouth moving, and then she crossed herself again and we went back to whatever we were doing. I thought she looked so beautiful and peaceful when she did that, like the paintings of Our Lady in the school oratory.

And I wished Bernadette was my mother instead, because she was never sick.

Three

Even though I had not liked the kissing bit at all, which left me having to wipe my face with the sleeve of my jumper, I had loved the moments before and after it when Dan had a big smile on his face just for me. He stood back just before he kissed me and really looked at my face and told me I was really pretty. Nobody had ever used words like that about me before. All my mother ever said was that I needed to cut my hair.

After the kissing, even over the summer when he had gone home and I did not see him, I used to spend a lot of time fantasising that he would marry me. We would live in a castle, and he would go away on the boat he always talked about. When he would come home he would run through the castle calling my name. Napoleon always did that on the television series I was into, looking for Josephine. When the next term started, I played that fantasy on a loop in my head on the way to school, and as I did the rooms in the hotel.

I had another scenario where Dan and me would go to see paintings in a gallery and stand together looking at them and then he would take my hand and kiss it.

Sometimes if I was doing the rooms by myself I would pretend the hotel was our house, and I would think about myself being Dan's wife, and that this cleaning I was doing was for him to come home to. If I was Dan's wife I would wear clothes like the pop stars, long striped skirts and platform boots. I'd grow my hair long and flick it out.

Niamh interrupted my daydreams one day, bustling in through the door with a pile of used towels from the opposite room to drop into the huge laundry bag on wheels that we pushed around. 'Did you tell Mr Murphy you're going to *London*?'

'I did,' I told her. 'You can train to be a chef in London.'

I had only said it to Mr Murphy for effect, but I wasn't admitting that. London was a place I thought you could probably train to be anything. But as I stood there, with Niamh looking so impressed at that idea, I decided that being a chef definitely was what I would do.

'I want to be a chef too, you know,' Niamh said, and we both stopped working and looked at each other.

'I'll be finished school before you,' I said. 'You're only in First.'

'Mr Murphy was saying it'll be a shame to lose you,' Niamh said, 'but you're not going soon, are you? You'll wait till you've the Inter?'

I straightened up. Niamh was taller than me but I was way older than her. I had prospects as well; Mr Murphy had told me I would do well in the industry. I *was* going to do my Inter Certificate the year after. It seemed a long way away, but I supposed I would have to wait.

'Anything to get out of here,' I said. I didn't really mean it. Ballyvourney was the nicest place we had ever lived. But I didn't know what to say, and I'd heard Carrie Power say the same thing last week. It sounded grown-up.

Niamh shook that comment off, blew her fringe away from her face. 'Maybe I'll go to London with you instead of school. My mam would let me,' she said.

I went quiet, but not because I didn't want her to. At that moment the idea of me and my best friend living together in London, in a place we could decide on – in a flat, where nobody would be shouting and where I could decide when I did the cleaning and when I could walk out the door and live my life without interference – that was such a dream.

'I think you're my best friend, Anne,' she said, then added the 'Marie' on the end hastily.

'I don't mind just Anne sometimes,' I said. 'Don't worry about it. Mr Murphy calls me that way a lot of the time.'

'He only ever calls me Moore,' Niamh said.

———

Our neighbour Maureen was in the house when I got home, just about to leave. She was folding papers she had brought about something and she looked me up and down and said to my mother, 'Does school not finish hours ago?'

My mother was a rare sight at home, but that day she was there at the table too. Both women smoked and there were stubs in the ashtray and my mother was tapping the ash off her cigarette, still in her work clothes. 'She works in the hotel,' Mam told Maureen, and put the flame to another.

I took a chance on something. 'Mam,' I said as sweetly as I could, 'my old skirt is getting a bit tight – I was wondering if I could buy a jean skirt? I'll use my own money and Niamh said she would come with me.'

'I'll go with you,' my mother said.

I knew I'd never get any jean skirt that way.

'I love the hair, Anne Marie,' Maureen said. 'It suits you longer.'

My mam had always kept my hair really short and discouraged it long. 'She looks wild,' she said now. 'It needs a cut.'

'Ah it's the style,' Maureen said, and winked at me.

My mother took a couple of drags on her cigarette before she answered, picking the specks of tobacco from her unfiltered Sweet Afton off her bottom lip with pincered fingers.

'She needs it cut,' she said.

I looked at the two of them sitting there, and then I went upstairs to my room.

———

On the way to work the next day some of the boys from my class were at the school gates. As I passed, Dan caught my eye and winked at me. 'Will I see you at the disco?' he shouted suddenly, even though he had been ignoring me all week.

I turned around. The boys he was with whooped and punched his arm for the laugh, surprised at his bravery. I didn't answer him, I was so surprised he called out. I just gave him a shake of my head and scurried the rest of the way to the hotel.

Niamh pulled me into a corner at the hotel as soon as she arrived. 'Come here to me.'

I looked over my shoulder back toward the dining room, where Mrs Murphy was on the warpath over double bookings.

'Hurry,' I said.

'I know you're going to London, I *know*,' Niamh said, 'but look.' She pulled a folded piece of newspaper out of her pocket and showed me, flattening it out on her palm and holding it up to my face.

'Wait,' I said, pushing it down to a good reading level. 'What am I to read?'

Her finger came across to an ad printed in the middle. She tapped it.

COOKERY SCHOOL, GALWAY, NO FEE, JOB GUARANTEED.

There was a phone number at the end to call. I looked at it and read it over and over.

'Galway?' I said. 'But we said London. Niamh, isn't that the plan?'

'No, I know,' Niamh said, 'but Mammy won't let me go to London – she said *this* is far away enough.'

'Galway,' I said again, thinking. I'd never been to London on my own, and the truth was I didn't even know the name of a course there or where I'd live. Having Niamh as a companion in Galway might be a better option.

I considered it all as I read the advert over and over, standing there in the hall of the Grand.

'My mam wrote to them, so we will see,' Niamh said.

I thought that was a bit premature, but I didn't know how to say so. My Inter Cert wasn't until next May, and Daddy might not even let me leave after that. He always went on about girls needing a good Leaving Cert. All the girls in his family had an education.

Four

A few days later, I was half-heartedly folding laundry while watching the television when I saw a car pull up outside. I stopped what I was doing, turned off the television and went to the door just in time for the knock.

Niamh and her mam were standing there, and there were two women behind them, fixing their collars and brushing their skirts down. They were both dressed very well and had their makeup done. Both wore white sheer tights with clean black shoes. One had dark-blonde hair, diamonds in her ears and a huge smile on her face. The other had red hair and seemed quieter and less flashy.

'It's ladies from the college in Galway,' Niamh said in a low voice, 'from the advertisement.'

And she pushed me gently out of the doorway and passed me into the sitting room.

'Hello ... hello,' I said to the strangers as they came in, but I was totally confused. I hadn't called about it, I hadn't written. What were they doing here?

Niamh's mother looked embarrassed as she passed, too. 'Sorry not to give you notice, Anne Marie,' she said. 'I mentioned to the ladies that you had an interest in the course so, well ... they thought "two birds one stone" sort of thing.'

Then everyone was inside of our house and I was shutting the door again, and turning so we could all look at each other.

They introduced themselves. Miss O'Rourke and Miss Smith, they said they were. They came forward to shake my hand before sitting down, and then we all sat, in a circle on the couches around the coffee table. I was fairly taken with their style: the clothes they wore were what I would have called 'high fashion' at the time.

Miss O'Rourke's hair was blow-dried in flicks around her face, like all the girls you'd see in the crowd on *Top of the Pops*. Miss Smith's hair was curly and shorter, and when she smiled you could see the black mercury of fillings in every tooth. I could see thick mascara on Miss O'Rourke's eyelashes and the silvery sheen of her green eyeshadow. Her lips glistened. They both wore pearls around their necks, and the material of their clothes was expensive, you could tell. Miss Smith's wool jumper was finely knitted. There was a diamond engagement ring on each of their ring fingers. I wondered what their fiancés looked like, and dreamed a little as I stirred tea in the kitchen for Mrs Moore. I had offered tea to everyone but it was declined by Miss O'Rourke and Miss Smith, they'd just had some, but I insisted, as you do, and then they all agreed to have a small cup.

As I went to make it I checked the window to see if Dad was coming. I knew he might pass the house for a pint in the pub. He sometimes did that on Sundays, especially if there was a big match. Mam was at work and would be for hours.

'Did you watch the match?' I asked when I returned with the cups of tea on a tray. Nobody answered that.

Miss O'Rourke supped her tea, and then she noticed a little chip on the edge of the cup and ran her finger over it and turned the cup around. I saw her lipstick stain on the rim.

'You're thinking of doing the course, Anne Marie?' she said.

'I'm going to go and do cheffing after my Inter Cert,' I said, 'if I'm allowed.'

Miss O'Rourke nodded. 'Well,' she said, '*we* don't require an Inter Cert to do our course, *and* we provide a full qualification – a diploma – at the end of training.' She turned to Niamh's mother. 'As I was saying to you, Mrs Moore, the girls will be fully qualified and *guaranteed* a job.'

One of my brothers blew in the door then, back from the big match, his coat hooked on to him by the elbow, flustered with the excitement of a win or a loss – it was hard to tell.

'Where's Dad?' he called as he came in.

'Over,' I hinted, and threw my eyes toward the pub. He took in the scene, widened his eyes at me and left.

'I'm going to work in the Grand after school,' I said suddenly, and then I didn't look at Niamh when I said, 'Mr Murphy promised me a job when I get a cert.'

I heard her gasp. 'Did he?'

'There's no work for *anyone* in Ireland,' Miss O'Rourke said, fixing her skirt. 'Really, who knows if a hotel in the middle of nowhere would even survive this recession?' She sighed and shook her head. 'It really is a gamble, isn't it?' Then she turned to Mrs Moore and said, 'At least our college guarantees that all students of our centre are placed in employment.'

Mrs Moore nodded very slowly and patted Niamh on the hand.

My dad arrived then, given the tip-off by my brother. He came in and took his coat off and hung it on the door. Then he turned to the room and raised his eyebrows as if to say, 'Well?'

'We are here to speak to your daughter, Mr Allen, and hopefully yourself and Mrs Allen, about the cookery course we run in Tuam,' Miss Smith said, standing up and holding out a hand, which he shook.

'I've never heard of this at all.' Dad looked at me.

I shrugged. I felt in the same boat.

'Right,' he said, looking at me and then at them, realising that this was serious, 'and you knock on doors usually, do you? Recruiting students?'

Miss Smith gave a little laugh. 'Not at all, Mr Allen. Mrs Moore wrote to us about Niamh when she saw our advert in the national papers, and when we were conducting our home visit there Niamh mentioned that Anne Marie' – she waved her hand to me – 'was interested as well.'

'I just said that I want to go to London some day,' I said again, 'to train in cheffing …'

'London!' My dad looked shocked to hear that. He took a minute to take stuff out of his pocket, placing his keys in the bowl by the door, and a few coins he had on the table. Then he turned to Miss Smith. 'Now, thank you both very much, ladies,' he said, 'but Anne Marie is coming up to do the Inter Cert next summer. Afterward she can look into this.'

'*Our* course is the equivalent of the Inter Cert, Mr Allen,' Miss O'Rourke said, confidently. 'You should consider this and think about it at least. Your daughter seems very suitable.'

He paused at that. 'And what college did you say this is?'

'Ballyglunin Park in Tuam,' Miss Smith said.

'And ye are qualified chefs, are ye?'

'We oversee our catering college,' Miss O'Rourke said.

'Sure,' my dad replied, twiddling his tie and smoothing it back, 'but with what organisation is it? Is it a university or a community college or what is it now?'

'A private college, Mr Allen,' was the response.

'With no fee?' he asked, sharp minded.

'No fee,' Miss O'Rourke said.

'And tell me,' my dad said, 'where on this good earth does the money come from to educate young women in the art of cookery if there is no fee?'

'*We* run our college ourselves,' Miss O'Rourke replied.

'*Ye* do,' my dad said, looking hard at her, 'and *who* are *ye*?'

'We are Opus Dei,' Miss Smith said.

My dad snorted and said, 'Ah!' as if he had found something out. He wagged a finger and shook his head and headed to open the door.

But my mother came in right then, tired and cold and wringing her hands. I could see she was in that humour she got into where she would go straight to bed in the dark and speak to nobody. When she saw all of us sitting there she looked like she might run back out, but Dad took her coat off for her and sat her down on the sofa.

'Anne Marie will get you some tea, love,' he said, going back to stand where he had been. He filled her in from there. 'These ladies are from Opus Dei, and they run a cookery course in Tuam, for chefs.'

My mam held onto the side of the couch.

'There is no fee for our course,' Miss O'Rourke repeated, smiling directly to my mother. 'Each participant gets five pounds per week while on the course, which is' – she turned back to Dad – 'in our Opus Dei centre in Tuam, County Galway.'

My mind filled with the thought of five pounds. I caught Niamh's eye and she raised her eyebrows. We couldn't imagine getting paid to get our qualifications. Sure we barely got half that amount working in the Grand, and there was no diploma at the end of that.

I knew the value of five pounds. I could get myself platform boots!

'Five pounds is a lot,' Dad said as I handed Mam her cup.

'There is an interview process,' Miss O'Rourke said then, turning away from my dad and fully addressing my mother. 'We don't accept *every* applicant. We vet each girl thoroughly to see if we believe they have what it takes to do our course. And this is a women's-only institution.'

My mother made a noise of satisfaction at that line and sprang to life. 'This girl,' she said, pointing at me, 'is a hard worker. Go down and ask the Murphys there in the hotel for a reference – they will talk all day to you about this one.' She looked straight at me and nodded as if something was solved.

That made me feel awful.

When Niamh and I told Mrs Murphy about the course that evening, she was suspicious. She kept bringing it back up with us as we rushed around serving and plating in the kitchen, looming up behind us, each time with a new question. We knew what she thought about it. She was visibly put out at the idea.

'A certificate is what ye want,' she said over and over again, with that delicious Cork intonation. 'Sure a diploma isn't worth the paper it's printed on to ye, mark my words.'

'She is just devastated to be losing us,' Niamh said, as she walked away.

That night in bed I felt a surge through me, a determination to go. It wasn't so much that I wanted to leave Ballyvourney – to be honest, I don't think I even thought about Ballyvourney. I just wanted to get away from the coldness in our house, and the cleaning and cooking I always had to do, and all the things I felt were unfair.

I wanted to be instantly independent, to be an adult.

It didn't matter that Mam clearly really wanted me to go, though I felt that, but I wanted to go regardless.

I felt, being young, that I would always be young and always be living at home, and that none of my beautiful dreams could ever happen if they didn't happen right now. I couldn't stand the thought. I couldn't stand it.

Five

Aunt Eileen was at our house the following day, sitting across from my mother, both smoking from a pack of Sweet Afton that was opened between them.

'Mrs Murphy doesn't want to lose good workers,' my mam said.

Nobody worked harder than Mrs Murphy, and she really cared for us and for the Grand Hotel. Nobody was there earlier and nobody stayed later. But I was used to my mother's way of seeing things, always making things negative. It was a habit she had.

It felt to me like Mrs Murphy was looking out for us because she wanted us to do well. And sure Mr Murphy had told me to come back after I qualified. Maybe I could do the course in Tuam and come back. Maybe by then I could live on my own here in Ballyvourney, or even Cork City.

My aunt hadn't tapped the ash from her cigarette once since Mam had started talking. 'Auntie?' I nudged her and brought her attention to it. She tapped it into the ashtray and took a last drag before she stubbed it out.

'Peggy, you can't let her leave school,' she said.

'Anne Marie, go on upstairs,' my mam said. So I did, but hung around on the landing with my ear cocked. I knew they would be talking about me.

'Eileen, you know what will happen a girl like Anne Marie if she stays around here,' my mam said. 'This course will be the best thing. An all-girls institution.'

'She isn't going to get ... you know she isn't that sort of girl,' Eileen said.

'You don't have daughters, Eileen,' Mam said. 'If you did, you would know.'

'Anne Marie is a good girl,' Eileen said, 'and clever. You can't let her leave school.'

'She is clever,' my mam agreed, '*but* she is the kind of girl to marry the first lad to throw a wink at her, I can see it, and that's nothing but an education wasted.'

'Is *my* education wasted then, Peg?' Eileen said. 'I'm married.'

My mother just shuffled her shoulders and smoked.

————

My dad was set against it. He called Opus Dei a bunch of weirdos.

'Do you really want your daughter instructed by religious nuts?' he asked Mam. 'Opus Dei are Franco's puppets.'

'Sure what would you know about Franco?' Mam was suddenly dead set on me doing this course, the answer to all her worries. Worry was what ate away at my mother when she wasn't feeling well. I hated to be worrying her. But I also hated these arguments. Hearing myself described as 'one of those girls' made my stomach knot up and my throat hot. I didn't know exactly what one of those girls would be, but *I* knew I was good. I wanted to be good.

My mother talked under her breath: 'Franco this and Franco that.' I turned on the TV but made the volume low so I would catch every word. Not that they were being discreet; they were talking about it as if I wasn't there at all. 'They're just Catholics like anyone,' she said, opening the window and steadying herself before switching on the kettle. 'Don't we go to Mass ourselves?'

'Opus Dei are severe in their religion, Peggy,' my dad said, and Aunt Eileen laughed out loud. 'You know as well as me Mass is our social thing, to see our friends and go up to the snug there after.'

Mam tutted and rearranged herself on the chair. 'Seán,' she said, 'you know as well as I do why this would be good for Anne Marie. What if Anne Marie gets into trouble?' She blessed herself. 'Is that what you want for your only daughter?'

I still didn't know what on earth she meant. What trouble?

'Opus Dei is a strict religious cult, Peg,' Dad said.

'Sure Jesus, Seán, the men that are up there teaching her every single day to read and write are a religious order!'

Her point was well taken. My dad sat down and poured tea into a cup from the teapot, stirred milk into it, thinking.

'Any other college will cost us money, sure that school costs us money,' Mam told him with her finger pressed into the table. 'This college is free, and on top of it, she gets paid, Seán.'

My dad stopped stirring his tea. 'That strikes me as odd, does it not you, Peggy? No fees? Payment? And what about her schooling?'

My mother flapped her hands at him, shooed the comment away. 'She has no interest, all that girl wants is fashion and music,' she said. 'Don't you know that?'

Dad was shut up by that. Maybe he thought she was right, maybe he thought she wasn't. He never said.

But *I* knew she was wrong. I loved fashion and music, sure I did, but I did want to be a chef.

'She is going,' my mam kept saying.

'Right, right,' Dad agreed eventually, and he and Mam went to the phone box in the village with his pen and paper and rang Miss O'Rourke on the following Monday. Mam dialled the number and held the phone out for him to take it, tutting at him because he was resisting. But of course once he heard Miss O'Rourke say, 'Hello?' he took the phone.

———

After the call, he told me we would all go to Tuam and it would give him the chance to suss these guys out.

My mother talked to everyone about it. She was right and Dad was wrong and Eileen was wrong and Bernadette was wrong on the phone from England, giving out stink over the idea that I would be let leave school.

'Well, Father Connolly thinks it's a great idea, Bernadette,' my mother said into the receiver after listening for what seemed like ages. 'You don't know everything, you know.'

A pause.

'Well, he said he would take account for them,' Mam said, 'so you don't know everything … No, no … you have no right to say that now, they were very well-spoken women … from Dublin!'

I couldn't hear what my aunt said next, but my mother responded, 'There isn't a job to be had in this country, and to be honest with you, Bernadette, I know your game – you want her to move to England where you are, all cosied up in that convent. You really haven't a clue, Bernadette, it's a hellhole over there for the Irish, why do you think we came home?!'

Something else was said then. Something sharp enough to have my mother gripping the phone, her face white.

'Well the interview is tomorrow,' she said, 'and we are all driving up to Tuam. Anne Marie might not even get a place.'

When she said that, I really hoped I would.

Mam hung up without saying goodbye. She turned on me straight after: 'Get out that door!'

I can't wait to get out of here, I said to myself as she closed the door on me, and I ran all the way to work and asked Mrs Murphy to put me on the evening service that weekend. Anything to get away from my house.

―――――

I was clearing ashtrays in the bar when Niamh came around the door calling my name, out of breath.

'They're on, Anne Marie!' she said. 'They're on now! On the radio!'

I knew who she meant, and we ran back to the kitchen just in time for the second verse of my favourite song.

'I told her to get you,' Tara shouted as me and Niamh swerved into the kitchen, and she turned up the radio, which was playing the song from the Levi's ad that we were all mad for. We all started dancing with each other, in the new style like the band did, arms out and hips banging together, turning a leg out and back – bump – and back, arms up – bump – there was such satisfaction in dancing like that. I loved it. I was a good dancer; everyone always said that about me.

Mrs Murphy wasn't long in turning the radio back down, shouting, 'We can't hear ourselves think here!' and then the news started and so we left the kitchen, splitting up to do the jobs needed under Mrs Murphy's watchful eye.

Niamh and me were *always* paired. 'You're quickest together,' Mrs Murphy always told us. Looking back, I would say it was that we were talking so much we just got the job done, and it was second nature to us by then.

'I'd say we would be great chefs,' I said to Niamh, as she lifted her end of a mattress and I lifted mine, pushing the top sheet under with a flat hand, smoothing it back into the crease and creating what Mrs Murphy called an envelope before dropping the mattress back down to hold it in place. Tight, but apparently not tight enough.

'When I say envelopes I mean invitations, not love letters,' Mrs Murphy told us, stepping in to show us how tight she wanted the sheets.

I wanted the good word. When she left the room I was annoyed with myself.

Niamh was chatting all the way down afterwards. 'Carrie says Mrs Murphy is a great boss, because she works with us, she does the same work we do, and gets down and cleans if the place needs it.'

I thought about that.

'Carrie says it's the sign of a good person,' she said, 'to be like that.'

I wanted to be talked about like Mrs Murphy was.

41

———

We all drove up to Tuam for the interview in the Moore family car. The two dads in the front, and the two mothers and two daughters squashed in the back. It seems impossible by today's standards to have travelled for so long like that, but it was how people did things.

My mother fell asleep against the window as soon as we took off for the four-hour drive to Galway.

'Have you a suitcase?' Niamh asked me on the way, and I shook my head. 'Me neither,' she said.

'You'll have to get one each,' Niamh's mam said.

'We haven't got into the course yet,' Niamh reminded her mother, but Mrs Moore shook that idea away and said we were both ideal candidates and of course we would get in.

We stopped in Ennis for lunch. There were starters and mains ordered, and we got egg mayonnaise, which for me at that time was the height of extravagance. I savoured every bite I took, looking forward to telling Mr Murphy about it as soon as I got back. Maybe I'd learn how to make it on the course.

Then we were served the main: pork steak and veg.

'Sure what do you call this?' Mr Moore asked in disgust, prodding his fork into a scoop of something on the plate.

'That's apple sauce for the pork,' the girl said, and went to lift the plate again, but he burst out laughing and in his thick Cork accent said, 'Lord have mercy, I thought it was a watery spud!'

Everyone thought that was hilarious.

'The potatoes are coming separately,' the waitress said. On our way out I gave her a small smile. I knew what it was like.

———

'It's this turn now, Liam,' my dad said to Mr Moore as we reached the last stretch, and the car swerved sharply in up off the road we were on and onto a smaller road. We could see high grey walls up ahead, and then a large gateway with red gates.

Mrs Moore reminded us all of the instructions. 'This is the back of the place. Through the arch, she said.'

Mr Moore brought the car around through a tight arch that led to a courtyard of cobblestones, surrounded with stables. Above the arch there were windows, and I wondered if those were rooms or storage. I noticed a set of two large windows in place of the stable doors at the end, and a door where Miss O'Rourke and Miss Smith appeared. Mr Moore pulled the car into a space Miss O'Rourke pointed out. We got out of the car.

This Galway air felt different to that in Ballyvourney and it gave me butterflies. It smelled different – more grassy than the hay-filled air we had at home, and there was a touch of something, salt maybe, that made it feel colder. It seemed fresher.

'Come in, come in.' Miss O'Rourke was beaming that smile at all of us one by one, but I felt like she caught my eye in particular and gave me a special look that told me, *you're the one*. I really felt that: the way this had all happened, the way they had insisted on coming to our house from Niamh's, it felt as though they *knew* something about me, that I was special – that I was going to be a great chef, maybe – and they could say they trained me.

This was something. I could feel it.

Dad huffed and puffed and remarked on the building and on the stables. I could see he was impressed. He and Mr Moore compared observations on the stonework.

'Georgian or Victorian,' my dad said.

'You're right, Mr Allen, a bit of both,' Miss O'Rourke said, and my dad was pleased.

I closed my eyes and breathed in the air and thought to myself that this was going to be my day, my time. I *would* get a place on this course, I *would*.

Six

Ballyglunin Park is a grand house with fields all around it. There are no hills, or forest even, to break up the horizon at all. I had expected the inside to be a certain way, with elaborate design and ornate workmanship, and I was looking forward to seeing it, but once we got inside we saw that it was as simple and plain as possible.

That was surprising.

There were three women to greet us: Miss O'Rourke and Miss Smith, who we had already met, and then a woman named Fionnuala O'Reilly was introduced briefly as she passed us in the hall. We were brought in and given tea in a large sitting room downstairs, with a huge window which used to be the stable door, and which looked totally out of place. There was nothing on any of the walls, except for a holy picture opposite the door, and the furniture was like something you'd find in a dull office, grey or brown and plain as day.

There was a huge press with a key with a gold tassel hanging off it. 'We have a television,' Miss O'Rourke demonstrated, opening the press to show off the set inside, 'but it is supervised access for our girls only.'

Dad approved. He gave me a strong side-eye.

'We also show approved films,' Miss O'Reilly said. 'Last week we watched *Arsenic and Old Lace* – it was very good.'

I winced. I was glad they'd already watched it. That was an old-person film. 'I wonder can we vote for what we watch,' I whispered to Niamh. We were sitting together on the settee.

Miss O'Rourke stood up then and gave a little clap. 'Mrs Allen, Mrs Moore,' she said, 'let us show you the students' bedrooms.'

My mam looked at her cup of tea halfway drunk and the plate of biscuits that she hadn't had any of, and paused, but then agreed – breaking a biscuit in half, eating it, and taking a good sip of tea before she got up and joined the others on a tour of upstairs.

'We *never* put two girls sharing a bedroom together,' I heard her say as they went up. 'Either one, three or five.'

My mother made noises of approval. 'You just never know with girls,' she said as she reached the top of the stairs, 'with all the revolting music they listen to these days.'

I could hear Miss Walsh speaking all the way down the hall, telling the women that we would be safe as houses there.

Miss Smith asked me if I was ready for my interview, and at the same time Miss O'Rourke told the dads that she would show them the grounds. Niamh was to wait in the sitting room; her interview would be after mine. I followed Miss Smith up the stairs.

I could hear my mother's voice from an open door, talking about how girls in Ballyvourney had to go to the boys' school with the boarders. The way she said it sounded awful. I heard Miss Walsh reply that girls had no care for themselves these days, and my mother agreed and said, 'Let me tell you ...'

I cringed hearing that. It sounded like she was blaming the girls in Ballyvourney, like we were bad for going to school with the boys. The way she said it, it sounded like it was our fault if we got killed or whatever it was that was worse than that.

'Now,' said Miss Smith, and she opened a door with a key, leading me into a small room that I realised was her bedroom. I was overcome with embarrassment and stared straight ahead as she sat down.

Her bed was oddly made: it looked really flat on top, and the bedding was folded oddly at the edges.

'What would you like to get out of the course, Anne Marie?' Miss Smith was smiling and leaning forward as she asked me. She smelled lovely. I looked around her dressing table to see if I could see a bottle, but there was nothing much displayed.

'I would like to be a chef,' I said, softly in order to sound serious. I couldn't stop looking at the bed. It looked like there was no mattress at all. Just a flat board laid across the frame, with a sheet wrapped on it.

'This is the place to learn cookery, Anne Marie,' she replied. 'What we offer here you will not find anywhere else: safety, good accommodation, training and a payment of five pounds a week!'

'That does sound very good.' I pretended to mull it over, as if I had a clue.

'The job market after school in Ireland is very difficult,' Miss Smith went on, 'and it's only getting worse.'

I'd heard people say the same. Everyone's goal in Ireland at that time was to get a job and keep a job. My dad sometimes said that to my brothers about the mill. So I nodded and repeated it. 'I want to get a good job and keep a job.'

'We ensure each participant is in full-time employment when the training is over,' she said.

'I'd like to work in a hotel,' I said.

'Yes, yes,' Miss Smith agreed, 'a job in residence would really suit you.'

I had never in my life been spoken to like this. Mrs Murphy spoke to us like teachers did, gave orders and gave out and was stern with us. We spent most of our time in the Grand trying to make sure she would be pleased with us. It was a comfortable place to be; I was used to that dynamic of the adult and the child. This weird reversal felt like Miss Smith was the one looking for my approval, like she was selling me something. It set me on edge.

'Now.' Miss Smith made some marks on her paper as if she was writing. I noticed they were plain little marks and there was no writing there at all. 'Have you any questions for me, Anne Marie?'

I thought about it. 'How many girls will be on the course?'

Miss Smith leaned back and looked really impressed. 'Well now, you have a very clever mind, don't you, thinking to ask that?'

I sat up in my seat. This woman could see in me something I thought about myself too.

'Anything else?'

'Do you teach us how to make desserts?' It was all I could think to ask.

Miss Smith widened her eyes, leaned right in and said in a low voice, 'I reckon you'll be *teaching* the course at the end of it, don't you?'

I gasped at that promise. 'Would I?'

She nodded, ran her tongue over her teeth and patted me on the hand. Then she stood up and so did I. 'Girls like you don't come along every day, Anne Marie,' she said. Then she leaned away as if to give me a good look. 'You've beautiful skin,' she said, 'and gorgeous hair.'

I pressed my lips together, unsure of what to say to that.

'Why don't you wait downstairs for me now, Anne Marie?' Miss Smith suggested, and so I went back down, meeting Dad coming in the door.

'Well now,' he said, with windswept hair and red cheeks, 'it's nippy out there. How did you get on? It's lovely here, isn't it? Did you do well?'

I did a half shrug, not wanting to say that I thought I had.

'No better woman,' he said.

'Anne Marie did excellently in her interview,' Miss Smith said, and she put a hand on my shoulder as we stood with him in the hall. 'Excellently.'

'Well now,' my dad said, 'this place is fantastic, now, so it is, a beautiful place to study.'

He had completely changed his tune, it seemed, after the walk.

Miss Smith ushered us into the sitting room again, where my mother and Mrs Moore were sitting. I sat down. My dad and Mr Moore checked the room. My dad knocked on the walls and said, 'Solid.'

'So ye are nuns, is it,' Mr Moore said, 'all of ye here?'

'They're not nuns, Liam,' his wife told him.

Miss Smith shook her head and smiled. 'No, we are *numeraries* of Opus Dei,' she told the room, 'unmarried celibate members who dedicate their lives to *the Work*. We facilitate the course here in this school.

'There are thousands upon thousands of members of Opus Dei worldwide,' Miss Smith added, 'and let me tell you that Opus Dei are a *very* important part of the Catholic Church. The new Pope himself has great love for Opus Dei and works very closely with our Father Don Álvaro del Portillo in his private quarters in the Vatican City in Rome.'

My mother looked very impressed. The new Pope was big news: we had all seen him waving on the balcony when he had been elected.

'I thought you were engaged,' I said.

'We wear engagement rings,' Miss Smith explained, and her voice sweetened into a girlish tone, 'to express our lifelong commitment to Opus Dei. We choose our own rings.'

I would have loved a ring like hers. It was a diamond with two blue stones either side, on a thick gold band.

'So none of ye are married?' my mam said.

'There are married members,' Miss Smith said, showing all her teeth as she beamed at us, 'they live with their own families, but the female "Super numeraries", married women, come here for their spiritual direction and get-togethers with us weekly.'

Then, Niamh came back from her interview with Miss O'Rourke, and she came back beaming.

'Did you get on well?' Mrs Moore whispered, and Niamh nodded and suppressed a smile. Her mother put her arm around her and squeezed.

'Well done,' she said.

'We will let you know if you've made it through on Monday,' Miss O'Rourke said. Then she leaned in and patted my hand

and said in a low voice, 'I have no doubt we will be seeing you both coming to Ballyglunin House.'

A blush rushed to my cheeks.

Miss Smith caught my eye and gave me a nod and a flash of a smile. 'Two exceptional girls,' she said.

I had never been called exceptional in my entire life. Not in school, not in work, and certainly never at home. But sometimes I *felt* exceptional, like when I was dancing with the girls in the hotel – even when we were just messing, I always hit the mark. And when I was doing the stuffing, I always got it right. 'You've a knack for that,' Mr Murphy would say. I had a feeling that I could be somebody exceptional, something other than this trouble Mam always made out like I was heading for. But she was no role model. She was always so unsettled.

I didn't want to be like that. I wanted a great job.

'May we show you the oratory?' Miss Walsh said, and we followed her. Outside of the oratory there was a large black cross that was the size of a person. I saw Dad catch Mam by the eye and flick his gaze to it so she would look too. She frowned and tutted at him to give it up. Just inside the door, there was a table with a box on top. Miss Walsh opened it and took a black lace triangle out and placed it on top of her head. I'd seen veils like that before: some of the old ladies in Ballyvourney wore them in Mass. Miss O'Rourke and Miss Smith put them on as well, and then we went in through the door to a large room that had been set up as a sort of church, with pews and an altar with a tabernacle at the top, an aisle down the middle, and to the side, when I looked, there was a Confession box. I wondered if we would get to use this oratory when we were students.

As soon as we entered there, something strange happened. It was like the women sank into themselves, with eyes glazed over and movements that looked slow and inauthentic, like they were putting on an act in a school play. Approaching the tabernacle in a trio, they sank down onto one knee in a deep curtsy, which they held for a few moments before standing again and blessing themselves with an appearance of thoughtfulness, touching their heads, their mouths and their hearts in slow deliberation, with their eyes closed and their mouths pursed tight.

I had never seen anything like it. I looked at Niamh, but she was staring at them with her mouth open and eyes wide, and I knew she had never seen anything like it either.

I felt an urge to copy them. The movement they did was so quiet and hypnotic.

Afterwards they made a big fuss of saying goodbye to us, singling Niamh and me out, making sure to say, 'We will see you very soon.' As we drove off they were standing in the courtyard, beaming and waving goodbye with their hands high up in the air. I had never seen such a send-off ever before.

'There's a television,' Mam said as soon as we got back into the car.

'We all saw it, Peg,' Dad said, turning in his seat.

'They said they play movies at the weekend as well,' Niamh said, excited as I was. We sat holding hands in the back.

'On a projector,' Mam said, 'just like the picture houses from years ago.'

I listened as they went on. Out the window the beautiful stone walls and patchwork fields went by as Mr Moore drove us home. I could imagine it so well: my thoughts were all about myself, free and studying in that beautiful house. I would return to Ballyvourney a qualified chef. I would be something. People would know me because someone would say, *There goes Anne Marie Allen, the famous chef from London.*

'They said to me that Anne Marie could end up teaching there,' Mam said.

I could feel the relief off Mam as she said that, and it hurt me, because even at 15 I knew you had to have a Leaving Cert to be a teacher. She knew I wasn't going to be a teacher, but for whatever reason, it seemed she needed me to be in this place. Maybe she just wanted me safe from whatever demons she had herself, but it hurt anyway.

Looking back, I believe those women could have told Mam I was going to be the next pope and she would have lapped it up, because they were taking me off her hands. That would be one worry down, one less thing to occupy her thoughts in the night.

———

A few days later we went shopping for suitcases in Cork City, and Dad bought me one in Dunnes and I filled it with all of my things. Then Dad drove me up to Tuam. I remember looking out the back window of his van, sitting on my suitcase, and seeing the rest of my family, and my puppy Fido, standing there, looking after me and waving me off.

I was surprised by that. I think I thought they wouldn't even notice I was gone, because I never felt like my presence meant anything in our house.

When we finally arrived, my dad brought my case in and everything smelled and felt new and foreign and exciting. I felt like I had jumped worlds, from the old humdrum to something incredible. I felt like my life was beginning with that scene, like a movie. I was starting something for myself. I was going to be somebody. When he drove away, Miss O'Rourke patted my arm which was crossed through the other, and she said, 'It's hard to say goodbye, isn't it?'

I nodded and lowered my eyes and agreed with her, but to be honest with you, I didn't give a shit.

Seven

There were other girls there when we arrived, and some more came later. We met Sharon Clark from Cork, shorter than any of us with a mop of thick brown hair and brown eyes, and Mary Flanagan from Cork too, taller than everyone with long blonde hair. They felt familiar because they knew Niamh through family.

She had sent them the details of the course too.

'She rang me about it three times in one day,' Sharon told me, 'convincing me to come.'

'Me too,' Mary Flanagan said.

Then there were two other Marys: Mary Wilson, a chunky girl with prominent teeth and really curly hair that she had cut into the shape of a bob, and Mary Donovan, from Clare, who wore cool platform shoes and had her hair long down her back in a plait.

We were shown bedrooms, three to one room, five to the other. I was sharing with Niamh and Sharon. 'Mam made sure we would be bunking together – she rang ahead,' Niamh told me, and we took the bunk beds in the room.

After putting our cases on our beds we went across the hall to the bigger bedroom where our classmates were. The room immediately erupted with all excited chatter, girls trying to get to know each other's names quickly, and we compared our notes on pop stars and movies and what we liked and who our favourites were and wore ourselves out in about ten minutes.

'Girls! The course begins immediately,' Miss Smith said, looking in the door. 'See you in 15 minutes.'

As we mooched around the house on the way down, looking for the kitchen where we were to meet Miss Smith for our first lesson, the walls and floors of it felt familiar, perhaps reminding me of the house I used to go to with my aunt Bernadette. I felt comfortable there. It felt like somewhere I could finally be myself, finally be liked and part of a gang.

And as we all came downstairs I knew I had an advantage. I heard the other girls whisper to each other that the kitchen was huge, but it was half the size of the one I was used to working in with Mr Murphy. There were one or two counters, a big six-ring gas cooker with ovens under it – big ones – and a big server. Then there was a dishwasher and a few sinks and the fridges.

I winked at Niamh. This was a piece of cake.

Miss Smith was in the kitchen, wearing a white coat over her fancy clothes. She opened the fridges as soon as we came in, and pulled out plastic bags of lettuce, tomatoes, cucumbers and a huge hunk of ham wrapped in paper. She put it all down on the worktop. Then she opened a drawer, took out knives and put those down. Finally she rooted around in a large paper bag that was on a bottom shelf and took out two onions and put those down. I felt a flip of excitement. What would she teach us? Probably something basic, but I was ready to learn.

'Now, girls,' Miss Smith said, clapping her hands, 'get this all chopped into a nice salad and I will be back in 20 minutes, all right?'

As she left the kitchen, I noticed her give a slow nod to the crucifix on the wall by the light switch.

None of us had ever been on a course before, and we had no idea how it should or would go. So we rowed in, all of us going for the knives at once, and then the ones who didn't get one just stood there while the vegetables were chopped up. One girl chopped big slices, the other small diced squares, and then they argued about that.

'She didn't say what way,' Sharon said.

I was just an onlooker – I hadn't got a knife – but I would have thought diced was more appropriate for a salad. So I said so.

'What would you know?' Mary Wilson asked.

'I work in a hotel,' I said, and put my chin up.

'So do I,' said Niamh, and took control of the knife and handed it to me. I chopped the rest of the vegetables faster than I would normally, wanting to show these girls who they were up against.

'Well,' said Mary Flanagan, handing over her knife too, 'we have some pros in the place.'

Me and Niamh got very serious then, calling out directions to the others, who ran around after us.

'Right,' I said, looking up under my eyebrows, as if I was Mr Murphy looking over his glasses, 'a large bowl, please.'

Someone ran and got one and I made the salad in it, showing the girls how the juice in the tomatoes would cover everything and so you just needed a spritz of oil, and a splash of vinegar and salt, to really make it tasty. The words I used were straight from Mr Murphy's mouth.

'They must be testing us,' I said then to Niamh, 'to see how advanced we are.'

'Anne Marie is very good,' I overheard Mary Donovan say to Mary Flanagan, and inside I felt like I was lifting off with pride. I suppressed my smile. I *was* very good. I knew I was in the right place. I was going to do this; I was going to be an expert chef.

Miss Smith came back in then, a bundle of white cloths under her arm, and I expected her to notice the good work we had done, this already-forming team that had brought this food all together so fast.

'Right,' she said, not even seeming to notice, 'plates are in here; you can set the table in the dining room upstairs now.' She checked her watch. 'And hurry up, it's nearly supper time.'

'Good,' Niamh whispered, as we all knocked into each other and skidded across the floor in our haste to be seen doing something. 'I am absolutely starving.'

'Just five plates,' Miss Smith said, holding up her hand as I pulled a whole pile out. 'This is just the setting for the dining room, which I will show you now.'

I was confused, but I put the plates back. This must be silver service training or something. I wished she would tell us.

And so we took five of everything and followed her in. She shook out the white cloth and pulled it onto the table that was in the middle of the room.

'Usually this seats eight,' she said, 'but it's only five of us for supper this evening.' She pointed at the extra chairs. 'Take those out of here now, Sharon.'

Sharon did as she was told.

Miss Smith showed us how to set the table, placing two forks on one side and a knife on the other with a soup spoon. She put a dessert spoon along the top.

'Some days,' she said, 'it will be a small fork up top, depending.'

She folded a napkin into a small triangle and placed it on the side plate, and on top of that a small butter knife. Me and Niamh looked at each other. This was what we did in the hotel.

'Always work clockwise,' Miss Smith told us. 'This is exactly what we want.'

She showed us where to place the silver salt and pepper shakers in the middle of the table.

She got a silver ladle and placed it at the top of the table, and told us the tureen was to go there. There was a small brass bell on a huge sideboard, and Miss Smith said it was not required for this meal, but in the future we were to place it on the table as well as everything else – in case we were needed.

I watched her intently, so that if she looked up she would see that I was paying attention and that I was eager to learn from her, even though I already knew all of this. This was stuff I'd never even been formally taught to do – I had just followed Mrs Murphy and done things the same way she did.

'Now,' Miss Smith said, 'set the rest of the table just like that, girls, and I will be back in 15 minutes.'

There were eight of us. In less than a minute we had set the table.

We stood waiting there, looking around, looking at the table, one girl straightening a fork, another moving it back. It was excitement and awkwardness and no real rivalry – we were all so pleased to get going. I imagined for all of us this process of coming to Ballyglunin Park had been as fast as it was for Niamh and me. It had been less than a fortnight since Niamh showed me the advertisement. Now I was here, living my dream.

Miss Smith clapped her hands as she came back into the room. 'Okay, girls, downstairs we go now, and I will show you how the supper is to be presented, and then you girls can clean the kitchen and eat yourselves.'

I was thrilled. I had looked at the backs of the knives and forks as I set them down, and they were stamped. I couldn't believe that I would be eating with such beautiful cutlery, and off such beautiful tableware. It looked like bone china – not that I had ever actually seen any.

Back downstairs, Miss Smith told us to lay out platters, two types, one silver plated and two others in stainless steel. She took scoops of the salad onto large sharing plates, and showed us how to lay out the salad in portions on one side and fold slices of ham in the middle.

'It's important to make food attractive,' she said, 'all right, girls?' And she cut up thick slices of bread, showing us how to measure the slice with the tip of the knife, and placing the slices into baskets, one with linen inside and the other two with paper.

She took a match and lit the stove, and then she let it go out and did it again to make sure we got the instructions well enough to do it ourselves.

'Soup!' she exclaimed, opening a huge vat of cream-coloured powder with green speckles, and scooping the powder into cold water. We watched it thicken as she stirred it to a fat, gloopy boil. She ladled the hot soup into large white tureens and covered them.

'Now,' she said, 'serving spoons and forks from the drawers, take the silver platters and put them on the table up above for the directors. The others go into your dining room. We will call you when we are finished, and you can clean up and eat your own supper.'

'Where do we eat?' Sharon asked, frowning, her chin pulled back.

'I'll show you the student dining room now,' Miss Smith said, and brought us through the back of the kitchen, down a corridor with an old phone box on the wall, into a basement room with windows high in the wall around the top. The windows were covered with a white plastic film except for one; that one had earth piled against it on the outside. It felt like a grave. The rough walls had flaky paint clinging onto them and the flagstone floor was splitting and coming up in places. The air felt cold and mouldy and there was a strong smell of must.

In the middle of that room was a square Formica table, like something pulled out as a spare, and it had old schoolroom chairs around it that had seen better days. There was no tablecloth, just stainless-steel knives and forks of all descriptions and paper napkins. There was a dresser with a plain white table at the side, and you could see black mould spreading behind it.

This was where us students would have our supper?

'Now, girls,' Miss Smith said, 'please lay this table for yourselves like you have been taught and once the serving upstairs is done you might serve yourselves. Thank you.'

I felt a sinking feeling in my chest. Many times I had been called to prepare and serve afternoon tea to guests in the hotel, and I often brought Mrs Murphy a cup of tea and some biscuits. But this felt different.

Sharon read my mind. 'Is this a bit weird?'

But before I could say anything Niamh whispered, 'This is exactly how you learn – on the job!'

I shrugged. I was confused. Everyone was – you could feel it. But some, like Niamh, were being optimistic. That wasn't my nature; I was straight to the worst-case scenario.

Sharon and I looked at each other.

'Right, come on, then,' she said, taking a hold of my arm.

We were on the same page.

―――――

After supper the Opus Dei directors came out of their dining room.

'Say hello to Miss O'Reilly, girls,' Miss O'Rourke said, not really looking at us. We nodded and said hello, remembering her from the interview.

'Mary was one of the first members of Opus Dei in Ireland,' Miss Smith said.

I said nothing, because that didn't mean much to me, but one or two of the other girls said *oh* with as much interest as they could muster. I looked at Sharon, who shrugged.

'Now clean the kitchen thoroughly,' Miss Smith said. 'I will run through the proper workings of that now tomorrow, but for now just clean it as best you can, so that you can get the dishes done and prepare the breakfast tables for tomorrow … Make sure to save all of the leftovers. Do not throw anything away.'

I nodded along, but I didn't understand.

'That will be your lunch for tomorrow,' Miss Smith said. 'No need to make more.'

I was appalled. There was never one day where Mr Murphy wouldn't feed his staff well with food he had cooked just for them.

'Sure you wouldn't give scraps like that to a dog,' Sharon said quietly.

My mind was working overtime and I could see some of the others' were too. I kept trying to read Niamh, and I caught her wrinkling her nose as we cleared the plates and were reminded to eat what was left. Never once had the Murphys served their staff from the leftovers; sure we would be offered cake to take home, or some of the meat to wrap up if it was left on the bone, but never off the tables, never ever leftovers from someone else.

When we had the kitchen scrubbed, we laid the tables and prepared the breakfast for the directors the next day – large bowls of cereal, milk in jugs, butter in dishes, all covered in cling film and left in the big fridge. I had never seen so much cling film used. We were told to use it on everything – on the bowls of cereal, the jugs of milk, the baskets of sliced brown bread, the butter dishes.

We were famished.

'I suppose a cooking school will have its own system,' I said as I picked through the leftovers.

Niamh nodded enthusiastically. 'We can't compare it to the Grand.'

'You just can't compare,' I agreed. 'That's a hotel, *this* is a school.

Eight

Miss O'Rourke and Miss Smith walked us around the various rooms in the house as soon as we were finished supper.

'You'll be working on these rooms every day,' Miss Smith said.

She must mean 'in', I thought at first.

But there were no boards to write on that I could see. There were no shelves, no books, no desks or even seats at tables. I couldn't see anything for study at all, although there were folders in the kitchen full of recipes clipped from magazines and put into plastic pockets. Maybe some of those folders had our study sheets as well.

Each time we came to a room I watched this ritual happening. The directors would nod toward the crucifix hanging there, and when they came up to a picture of the Holy Family – and there was one in most rooms – they took a moment to nod to it as well.

'This is all a bit mad,' Sharon whispered as they led us down to the oratory, where each of them kissed the black cross that was hanging on the wall there. 'What have you signed us up for, Niamh?'

She said that over her shoulder, as Niamh was walking behind. It was a dig.

I looked over my shoulder and gave Niamh a little smile. Her cheeks were roaring red. She narrowed her eyes at Sharon's back as we went along, so I stayed behind to walk with her instead. Sharon was surely jumping the gun a bit; even though I was feeling the same way, at least I was sure it would all start soon.

'We have Mass here every morning,' Miss O'Rourke said. 'To enter *we* wear a mantilla' – she reached into a drawer in a side table and took out the thin lace headdress – 'and *we* cover our head. But of course you girls don't have to.'

She laid the lace triangle on her head and led us into the oratory and immediately her facial expression went, like it had at the interview, from a smile to serious and sombre. Miss Smith did the same.

The tabernacle in the oratory was a brass box, with a gold key in the lock and a large gold tassel hanging off that, and as they approached, their body language shifted. They almost floated themselves up the aisle of the oratory to the tabernacle and genuflected right down onto the floor. They really bowed when they did this, dipping down on a crossed leg. I liked the way they looked doing that. It was graceful. It reminded me of how women in the period dramas I loved curtsied.

I really loved the look of the mantillas and of their beautiful floral clothes, and the way their hands crossed on their knees as they went down. It was all so ladylike.

————

The next morning I woke to the sound of Miss O'Rourke knocking on our bedroom door, telling us quietly it was time to get up and reminding us that Mass was at seven-thirty. She looked like she had been up for hours, tired around her bloodshot eyes. Her hand kept wandering to her neck and rubbing the skin there.

'Did you sleep well?' I asked.

She laughed a little and shook her head. 'I did,' she said, but I did not believe her.

The Mass that morning was the first I went to in Ballyglunin.

When I went in, the Opus Dei women were already there, and it seemed that they were in deep meditation. The girls and I sat in the back pews. I heard a swish and looked around, and a tall man wearing a long black cassock and the usual priest collar came through the room. He looked at no one, sweeping across the parquet floor into the sacristy. A minute later he appeared again, wearing a white alb and his vestments to say Mass.

He walked across to the altar and stood with his back to us.

I looked at Sharon and she at me with her eyebrows raised. The priest began to say the Mass with his back to us, chanting loudly in Latin, words we didn't know and couldn't respond to with the Opus Dei women, who knew every word.

'Is that Latin?' Sharon whispered, and I nodded. I had taken it for a year in First.

The priest only turned to give the Communion. We all walked up, Sharon ahead of me and Niamh behind me. Sharon held up her hands to receive, one under the other. The priest stood looking at her blankly and brought the Communion to her mouth. Embarrassed, she opened her mouth, and he laid it on her tongue. I saw that, and so I just went straight for the open-mouth approach. On my way back down, I saw Niamh raising her hands higher and higher before she gave in and opened her mouth. I understood. Being fed Communion was so humiliating.

When it was over we skipped outside to giggle.

'Sweet Jaysus,' Sharon said, 'he nearly stuffed it into my throat.'

'My mammy takes it like that,' Niamh said, 'into the mouth.'

'Latin Mass,' I said. 'Brother Dominic would love that – loves the Latin.'

I caught Miss Walsh's eyes as she flashed them our way. She raised a finger to her lips. I poked Niamh so she would see it, and we stopped talking.

Down in the kitchen, Miss Smith appeared with her white coat over her clothes again. 'Now, girls,' she said seriously, 'boil the kettles and start making the toast. We will use these holders upstairs, these downstairs, all right?' She lifted silver in one hand, stainless steel in the other.

We poured hot water into silver tea and coffee pots for the teachers and stainless-steel pots for us. The other teachers appeared from somewhere once the breakfast was ready. Miss Smith took off her white coat, joining the other teachers as they went into their dining room, and we went into ours.

Then Miss Smith called us to follow her and we did, to a bare room in the stables, where there were folded dresses piled high on a table.

'Choose your size, girls,' Miss Smith told us, and pointed, and so we went and started looking through them, checking the labels and holding the dresses up against us. They were green, each with a zip up the front and a small pocket.

'Are these nurses' dresses?' Niamh whispered, running her finger over a large tea stain on the front of one.

I shook my head. 'Nurses wear white or navy,' I said. I knew that because my mother had trained as a nurse.

'They're a bit dirty,' Sharon said. She picked one up and put it down again so we could see a large dark stain on the hip. She picked up another and turned it back and forth.

Niamh held hers to her chest defensively. 'Well, it is a kitchen with sauce and oil,' she said. 'It's practical wear, not fashion.'

'Would you go on, and you working in a hotel for ages,' Sharon answered her. 'You should know a good boil would get stains out – they clearly didn't try.'

Niamh stuck her chin out.

'I feel ridiculous,' Sharon said when we tried the dresses on. She shook her head as she leaned in to me. Her uniform was huge on her, hanging in folds like a tent, way beneath her knees. Mine wasn't much better.

'Sure I'm fit for camping in this,' I whispered back, and made her laugh.

I looked up and caught Miss Smith's eye, and she didn't smile at me even though I was smiling. She looked seriously displeased. My smile dropped and I stood up straight. I didn't like how I felt seeing her face like that at all.

'Thank you for the uniform,' I said. She nodded a 'You're welcome'. When I turned back Sharon was looking at me, amused.

None of the uniforms were ironed; the creases were hardened into them so that even when you'd been wearing them for a whole day they were still bent out of shape. There is something so degrading about creases, and I found myself trying to smooth them out through the day as if I could iron the dress solely with the heat of my hand.

Next, Miss Smith led us all upstairs into a bedroom, where in the middle of the floor there was a hoover, and a pile of bed linens on top of a basket.

'Can everyone hear me?' she asked, going onto her tippy-toes to look over our heads into the hall, to make sure there was nobody lagging behind. 'We all in? Okay.' She pulled at the bed linens, removing a sheet, then bringing it over to an unmade bed and shaking it out.

Mary Flanagan leaned in to me, and I turned my ear her way. 'Are we getting taught how to make a bed?' she whispered.

I nodded. It appeared we were. 'I could do that in my sleep,' I whispered back. These girls needed to know how much experience I already had. I did not need this basic stuff.

Miss Smith told us to move every piece of furniture, hoover under and behind and lift each piece back. 'Lift, not pull, the furniture,' she said. She stood at the wall and watched us doing it, occasionally fluffing a feather duster on top of the sideboards and pictures.

'Always go clockwise around the room,' she told us. 'Everything clockwise, all right, girls? And every room, every day,' she said. I heard Niamh gasp. Cleaning this entire house every single day seemed mad to me and I knew she would feel the same. Hotel rooms where people stayed were cleaned every day, of course they were, but we never had to go into the detail expected here – for rooms that were barely used at all.

But by the time the lesson was done, Niamh had reverted to defensiveness.

'It's part of hospitality,' she said as we went back down to the kitchen to prepare the lunch. 'In a hotel everyone has to know how to do everything.'

I nodded, but I didn't know what to think about that. This was a cookery course, not a housekeeping course. But I didn't say anything, because Niamh was looking more and more upset the more the girls complained.

In the kitchen Miss Smith showed us where to find the recipes for the lunch. They were in the huge folders on the shelf. We were shown where the ingredients and the utensils were and told to get going on dinner after lunch was over. We were to always follow the instructions in the recipe.

'Tonight there is only three for dinner upstairs,' she said, 'and the eight of you downstairs, so put on a few extra potatoes and carrots for yourselves, but we will use the leftovers first for your lunch, all right?'

Then she left us there, saying she would be back in a while.

'Chicken supreme with mashed potatoes,' I read out loud from the sheet left for us on the counter. Everyone looked at me for direction.

'Okay,' I said, feeling a surge of confidence. 'I will need flour, butter and milk for this sauce.'

Everyone sprang into action again, a room full of enthusiasm and hopefulness, all of us thrown by the fact that there were no lessons happening, but wanting to give this our all anyway. If we worked hard, and followed the instructions, surely it would work out.

———

'Everyone is going mad that you left school,' my brother Tony said, when he rang the next night. 'Everyone is asking Dad about it. He told them to feck off.'

I didn't like hearing about this.

'Mam told Maureen to mind her own business,' he said.

There was a pause.

'That crowd, though …' he said, 'they sound a bit mad, Anne Marie. Moriarty was telling everyone the Opus Dei lads whip themselves into a frenzy and all sorts.'

'That's ridiculous,' I said, but there was something about that line that rang true.

'They do so,' he said, 'they're known for it – a friend of John Forsyth's knew a fella who knew a man who was in Opus Dei and he beat himself so hard he bled to death. Or nearly did.'

John Forsyth was a boarder in my class.

'How do you know that,' I said, 'about what John Forsyth knows?'

'Sure the whole class was talking about you,' he said, 'running off to Opus Dei, Anne Marie, it's a hot topic.'

'I have to go,' I said.

'Auntie Bernadette rang Mam at work looking for you the other night,' Tony said, 'and she hung up on Mam when she told her you'd left school.'

I put the phone down.

Auntie Bernadette would want me to have further education; she always said that. I was going to get one here. I knew Bernadette would be pleased with this place. It was just like the convent we went to on our holidays, full of crucifixes and books about God. It was holy here and there was Mass every morning. I was never so holy or good in Ballyvourney as to go to Mass every day. I knew there was no way Bernadette would be against these people – sure weren't they like nuns themselves, the way they gave up for God? My brother had it backwards.

There was nothing wrong with Opus Dei. The Pope was friends with your man del Portillo sure, and wrote all about how good they all were in his letters. Everyone loved the new Pope. His picture was hanging all around the country. We had one at home, and there was one in Mrs Black's window across the way.

There was *nothing* wrong with Opus Dei.

———

The numeraries had explained the whole thing to us in what they called a 'get-together' in the evenings. There were five celibate women living at Ballyglunin. There was Miss O'Rourke and Miss Smith who called themselves our tutors. Then there was Miss Diaz who worked in Clare and drove every morning from Galway and Miss Byrne who would sometimes be staying there, we were told. They were introduced to us and often came to these meetings in the evening. And of course we saw them at Mass.

Miss Diaz scared me from the start. She had black hair and sallow skin that was grey under her pale blue eyes, and when she looked at you she seemed vacant like she was somewhere else, like she was a ghost. Her clothes were less colourful in comparison to the others and she rarely spoke. But she was always looking at us with this expression that looked almost like hate.

'Opus Dei is a global organisation,' Miss O'Rourke said. 'It is part of the Catholic Church.'

Sharon piped up and said she had been helping out at the Legion of Mary a good bit, and she thought it was similar.

Miss Diaz's eyes flashed when Sharon said that.

Miss O'Rourke looked a bit put out too, but said maybe it was in a way. '*But* in Opus Dei,' she told us, 'we have married members, called supernumeraries, and numeraries, who are unmarried celibate members, and we have members called assistant numeraries, who work and live and do the day-to-day without which the Work could not be fulfilled – assistant numeraries are the most special members of Opus Dei. Without them we could not function.'

'Are you an assistant numerary?' Mary Donovan asked.

The women shook their heads and laughed, looking at each other as if it was a crazy question.

'No, no,' Miss Walsh said, 'we have no assistant numeraries living at Ballyglunin.'

'That's right,' Miss Smith said. 'We are *numeraries*: we are unmarried celibate members of Opus Dei.'

Miss O'Rourke had held up a glossy magazine. There was a photograph on the front.

'This is our Father, our Founder,' she said, handing the magazine to me.

The photograph was of a priest. He had glasses on and was slightly balding. He looked far too normal to be a founder of anything. I flicked through.

'This magazine is for Opus Dei members *only*, so please look at it and hand it back to one of us when you are finished.' Miss Smith snarled the last bit and I gasped, closing the magazine and passing it to Mary Wilson beside me.

'Our Founder was Josemaría Escrivá de Balaguer,' Miss O'Rourke said, 'who founded the Work in 1928. The Father was a Catholic priest, actually, and there are tens of thousands of members in the world today who are Catholic. "Opus Dei" is Latin for "The Work of God", that is, the work of its members, which is to live the Gospel in the world, to transform the world by living *in* it, not outside of it – in a convent, for example.'

I could have sworn she looked straight at me when she said the last bit and I felt a pinch. She knew my aunt Bernadette lived in a convent. But my aunt Bernadette was out in the world every day; most nuns were. Bernadette had a job too!

'Nuns have jobs,' I said, but Miss O'Rourke didn't hear me.

'In Opus Dei,' Miss O'Reilly explained, 'we know that each person has a special purpose, a vocation, to help people live their Catholic faith through their daily work. We know that God wants every person to become a saint.'

I was surprised to hear that. A saint? Wow. Being a saint was a big deal – that got you made into statues. I wondered if Miss O'Rourke and Miss Smith would be saints.

'Opus Dei is waiting to be formally approved by the Pope as a Catholic organisation,' she went on, 'and there are over seventy thousand members worldwide.'

The magazine reached me again and I turned it over in my hands. 'Noticias' was written on the front.

'This magazine is for our female members only, and we receive it every two months,' Miss O'Rourke said.

I turned it over. On the back there was a photo of a dead body, the same man as on the front, laid out in state in a coffin. It made me feel upset to see that picture without a warning. The way his mouth sagged and his eyes were sunken down frightened me. I passed it on straight away.

'In our Work,' Miss O'Rourke said, 'our Father teaches us that learning to love others is to love God; it is the most important thing we do.'

'Being in Opus Dei is wonderful,' Miss Smith said. 'It's a big family, our family.'

'To live like a saint is to *be* a saint in ordinary life,' Miss Diaz said. 'It is the key to being happy.'

The others nodded emphatically when she said that.

There was a warm pause while they beamed at each other. Then they each turned their faces back to the room and beamed at us.

'Now, girls,' Miss Smith said, 'will we formally introduce ourselves and say where we are each from?'

I remember nothing really of that until it came to my turn. I had been repeating what I would say over and over as each girl took a turn. 'My name is Anne Marie Allen,' I said, 'and I am originally from London in England.'

Miss Smith's eyebrows shot up. 'Well,' she said, 'isn't that interesting? What can you tell us about London?'

My mind went completely blank.

What could I tell them? I had no idea. I used to live there and go to school and sit in a cold, empty house waiting for my parents to get home, just the same as I did in Ballyvourney.

'There's a big square full of blackbirds there,' I said. The room went silent.

'Blackbirds?' Miss O'Rourke leaned forward, looking confused.

I nodded. 'In London.'

Sharon Clark burst out laughing. She was an inner-city Cork girl and her accent blasted you when she was having fun, but right then her fun was at my expense and I wanted to die. 'Do you mean Trafalgar Square, girl?' she said, and pointed at me as she threw her head back and laughed out loud. 'Those are pigeons!!'

The entire room burst into laughter.

'Blackbirds!!' Mary Flanagan said, over and over. 'You mean pigeons!'

I nodded. 'Yes, sorry, pigeons.' I was willing them to stop and move on, but the laughing went on and on and on.

'Oh now, girls,' Miss Smith said with a clap of her hands, 'it's an easy mistake. Birds are birds.'

I kept my eyes fixed on the floor. Sharon poked me and I heard her say, 'Sorry,' but I didn't look up at all.

The others introduced themselves and there was a little bit of chat here and there about where people were from and what they got up to.

'Mass is daily in the oratory,' Miss O'Rourke said, standing to wrap things up, 'if any of you would like to go.'

She looked at me, lowering her chin as if to say, *Well?* I liked the feeling of that, being singled out.

'I'd like to go,' I said loudly.

'Great girl,' Miss O'Rourke said, and she came to sit beside me. Miss Smith talked about lights out and breakfast and the grounds, instructing us clearly that we were never to go outside without one of them.

'That is very important,' she said. 'We are your guardians *in loco parentis*, and you must not disobey the rules of the house here. Okay, girls?'

There was a murmur of agreement.

'You've lovely skin,' Miss O'Rourke suddenly said in a low voice, leaning into my space. 'Make sure to use rubber gloves doing the washing up –' she patted my hand '– don't ruin your nails.'

On the way to bed Mary Flanagan kept ribbing me. 'We better not leave you to recipes, Anne Marie,' she said, 'or we will be getting four and twenty blackbirds in our pies instead of chicken!'

I imagined pushing her down the stairs. But I held the thought back and chastised myself internally and held the door for her instead. I told myself I would emulate these saintly women and be the bigger person. But it was hard.

As I lay in bed that night I thought about my aunt Bernadette. She lived like these women, celibate and devoted to God. But she never wore nice clothes. I loved my aunt Bernadette, but when I saw the outfits she had to wear I knew I could never be a nun. I would much rather be the type of holy person that the Opus Dei women were. At least they could have the fashion.

Miss O'Rourke and Miss Smith were nothing like nuns, that was clear. They wore lots of makeup and fancy clothes, where Bernadette kept her hair hidden and wore no makeup at all.

My auntie was more holy than these ones for sure.

But then I thought about Ballyvourney and the Grand Hotel and I felt real excitement in my body at the prospect of a grand return. I was going to train here, and do well, and return to Ballyvourney in the latest fashion, with long hair and new shoes, a qualified chef, to work for Mr Murphy and never spill a drop of gravy.

Nine

'I just don't get this,' Mary Donovan said what we were all thinking. 'This is supposed to be college, but it feels like a full-time job.'

'Or slavery,' Sharon said. We had been in Ballyglunin a couple of weeks already.

We all felt the same way and we exploded, all talking at once, complaining and commiserating. Except for Niamh, who looked really annoyed at what was being said.

Miss O'Rourke walked through the door and clapped. We shut up and gave her our attention.

'Girls, girls,' she said, 'tomorrow we will be splitting the group and three of you will begin training in our centre in Gort Ard this week. The rest of you will go next week, and we will be going week to week like that. A fantastic woman named Miss Boyle will be coming to instruct you.'

My heart lifted. Now I could see that these few days had been about getting to know this house, where we would live. We *were* getting training. I looked over at Niamh. She looked delighted.

'A bus will come in the morning at eight-thirty sharp,' Miss O'Rourke continued, clapping her hands to a beat as she spoke. 'Straight after Mass, have a quick breakfast. Tomorrow's group, the first group to go, will be Niamh, Anne Marie and Sharon.'

I was thrilled to be paired with those two.

'Well, I'm not getting up for Mass,' Sharon said, really loudly. 'I'll see you at breakfast. I'll go to Mass Sunday ... maybe ... but I am taking all the sleep I can get. I'm already exhausted. I'll leave the praying to the Holy Marys.'

I turned my head and saw Miss O'Rourke stop in her tracks for a second, but she didn't turn around.

———

Gort Ard turned out to be a similar kind of stately home to Ballyglunin, just a bit smaller. Miss O'Rourke told us it was where the male numeraries lived, and that male students who attended university in Galway could live there.

We didn't go for training there. We didn't go for instruction or cookery classes. We learned nothing in Gort Ard.

We *worked* there.

The fantastic teacher, Miss Boyle? She was our overseer only. Over there it was nothing but the same routine we did in Ballyglunin. Oh, but we also ran a laundry.

Each morning our team of girls was split in two, and three of us would be driven to the men's residence by Miss Smith in the school's green minibus.

That first day, we were shown the laundry – much bigger and fancier than the smelly, mouldy washing machines at Ballyglunin. In Gort Ard there were bags of laundry instead of baskets, and each one had letters embroidered on it.

Miss Smith showed us the ropes. 'We' – she said as if she would be doing it as well – 'must empty each laundry bag and separate each item, socks, underpants, vests ... This is the basin for handkerchiefs.' She held it up. 'Now, Anne Marie, good girl, come here to me, now this iron here goes with this ironing table ...' and she tugged me across to look at this machine that we were to feed the sheets and tablecloths through.

'We are some eejits,' Sharon said, following the instructions with a grimace on her face, clearly put out like us all at this con.

'And girls, remember this is the *men's* centre,' Miss Smith said, and then looked around at all of us. 'You girls are *not* to speak to anyone here, do you hear me? We stay here in this section, the Administration, except when we do the cleaning between nine-thirty and midday, all right?'

The Administration. What a word to cover the kitchen, servery, laundry and dining room. But that was what it was called.

As we toured the rest of the house, we were shown double locks and bunches of keys that opened and closed doors into where the men were. These were the areas we were to stay out of. These were corners we were never to turn.

'Do you understand me?' Miss Smith said. 'Under no circumstances are you to go inside of there. You can only go in at the appointed time and with one of us. We will unlock the door. And if you see anyone, you look away and do not speak to them.'

We turned a corner right then, and suddenly there was a young man walking toward us, dark skinned and clean cut, with trousers rolled at the hem showing perfect white socks. Niamh clutched my arm.

'Oh!' the young man exclaimed and turned on his heel, while Miss Smith – as she had instructed – covered her eyes with her hands and stopped in her tracks.

I immediately did the same as Miss Smith, and when I took my hands down Sharon was looking at me like I had ten heads. 'Never seen one of them before?' she said, prodding me and making me giggle. 'It's a maaaaan.'

Miss Smith turned us back immediately and ran ahead of us in a panic, back into the Administration. It took her a minute to compose herself.

'Now, girls,' she said, with one hand on her chest and the other waving us in, gathering us around some boxes of cleaning equipment, 'I know what girls like *you* are used to, but this is an Opus Dei centre.'

Sharon's face darkened. Later she would give out yards about that comment. '"Girls like you"?' she said. 'How dare she make any sort of assumption?!'

We made lunch for the male residents and served it in the dining room. Once we exited, we could hear the doors being unlocked and the men streaming in to eat.

'Two of you will serve the men at dinner,' Miss Smith said as we locked the door behind us, 'and you will keep your eyes down when you do, all right?'

Next Miss Smith showed us the cleaning baskets – one for bathrooms, one for sitting rooms and bedrooms – then pulled out some coloured cloths and polish and held them up. We looked on the table in front of Miss Smith. Feather dusters, polishing cloths, sponges, scrapers and all sorts of equipment.

'How many times a week do these get used at home?' she asked.

'Once!' Niamh said loudly.

'Trick question,' Sharon said, prodding the air with conviction. 'It's all different – sure polishing can only be done once a month or you'll ruin the wood.'

Miss Smith wrinkled up her nose.

'In Opus Dei we have a saying: Clean Places, Happy Faces,' she said, but she didn't look happy at all. 'Here we believe that in order to live a good life you must have a clean home, and so this' – she waved the polish – 'is an everyday task.'

My heart sank. I hated polishing.

'We do the little things, the little things done well,' she told us. I wondered what she meant.

Sharon sighed really hard.

'And,' Miss Smith went on, 'that goes for all tasks. If you think there is a hierarchy of tasks, you are wrong: in Opus Dei centres we don't think, "What needs doing here?" We expect all things to be cleaned thoroughly and daily, as if it was spring. Every day. All right?'

I instinctively shook my head, and then checked myself quickly and nodded. Niamh's jaw was on the floor, and Sharon was stunned as well.

After lunch we brought all the platters back into the kitchen. There were odds and ends left of the chicken and salad sandwiches we had made for the men scattered on various platters.

'Waste not want not,' Miss Smith said cheerily, directing us to scrape everything into one bowl. She handed a whisk to Sharon. 'Whip a couple of eggs there for me, good girl.' She poured the egg Sharon handed her in on top of the chopped-up sandwiches, which she had scooped into a deep dish.

'Now,' she said cheerily, 'pop it in the oven and then we can slice it up for our lunch, all right?'

Our. She didn't mean that word, she meant *your.* We were eating slops again.

Half an hour later Miss Smith sliced the sandwich cake up and placed triangles of it on a steel platter. She sprinkled dried parsley over the top.

'Enjoy,' she said, pushing it forward, before stepping out into the other room.

Many of the leftovers in that thing were crusts, or old sandwiches, not eaten by the male residents upstairs. Even to me – ravenous by the time it came out of the oven – it was revolting.

'Jesus.' Mary Donovan took one look and walked straight over to take down the box of cornflakes. 'No bloody way,' she said.

'I'll have some of those too,' I said.

But Niamh took a slice, and she ate it.

'Lovely,' she said afterwards, but I had noticed her pause mid-chew a few times.

Miss Smith came back then to show us our dessert. She took a plate of cake leftovers and chopped it up. Then she shook icing sugar all over the top.

Sharon rolled her eyes.

'Sharon,' Miss Smith said, 'you'll be waitressing this evening, with ...' She looked around and I stood up straight. 'Niamh!'

I was disappointed.

Using Sharon as the model, Miss Smith showed us how to serve. We were to carry the big platter on our left hand, balancing the large serving spoon and fork on the end. We were to bend gently down to the men on their left, and point the serving spoon at them so they could serve themselves each portion.

'Do not go in too close,' she told us, demonstrating the distance by sitting Niamh onto a chair.

'And always remove the delph from the right,' she said, and reiterated the most important rules – to never look at the men and to keep our eyes down. 'If they need something,' she warned, 'they won't ask you; they will ask the director and he will ring a brass bell, all right?' She told us the sign of a good waitress was that bell staying silent all through dinner. 'They should already have what they need.'

Not long after that, Sharon and Niamh went ahead upstairs and I stayed in the kitchen. Miss Smith left me a list of what to get ready for the men's late-night supper and for their breakfast the next morning.

It was around nine o'clock when we left Gort Ard in the green bus to go back to Ballyglunin.

―――――

On our second day we were joined by Miss Boyle, who Miss Smith had said was there to instruct us. We were delighted to hear it. But of course she was not there to do anything but make sure we worked hard, and once we realised who we were dealing with our delight faded fast.

Miss Boyle arrived onto the green bus that morning in a skirt, cardigan and blouse, all perfectly ironed. And as she got on she ignored every single one of us.

'Get to it,' she said as soon as we arrived and disappeared into her office for the day.

So, that was how it was.

Every single day of that 'course', this small team of eight girls cleaned and scrubbed two large houses. The windowsills, windows, walls and skirting boards. The floors, the stairs, the banisters, the picture rails. The chairs, the tables, the shelves and units. The breakfast dishes, the lunch and dinner dishes, the platters and trays. The mountains of cups.

Every single day we would dust for cobwebs that were never there with a large feather duster. We would move all the furniture out to hoover the clean carpet underneath. The hoover marks from the day before would still be on the stairs, but we were to hoover it again anyway.

We washed every board of the floor with a wet mop and dried and polished it. Every bathroom was cleaned thoroughly, every toilet bowl, every tile, every panel and door scrubbed, washed down and dried. Each sink was left sparkling.

Three of us in one building, five in the other, lugged vacuum cleaners, cleaning baskets, buckets, mops, rubbish bags and laundry bags up and down those stairs, and we had to do it in total silence so as not to disturb the residents.

In Gort Ard – in the kitchen, servery and laundry – the counters would be cleaned and sterilised *every single day*. We

86

collected and lugged the bags of laundry from the bedrooms as we turned them over, and then we would wash everything and replace the bags in the same bedrooms a few days later.

We acted like unseen sprites, like in fairy stories, magically making the men in Gort Ard's lives hassle free, without even a thanks.

And after their late dinner and conversation the men left to go into the residence, so we would come in and clean the dining room again and set it out for their breakfast, ready for them in the morning, and leave out a full supper of sandwiches, cakes, drinks, tea, coffee and juices, all covered in cling film.

Then we would leave the kitchen immaculate and go back to Ballyglunin to sleep.

Ten

Gort Ard was a hard slog. Every week we would switch teams, three at Gort Ard, the others left at Ballyglunin. It was tough going for all of us, but the weeks at Gort Ard were the worst. It was occupied by young guys going to college in Galway, members of Opus Dei and mostly from Spain. They were immaculate, in crisp pressed trousers and shirts, but their habits were bad and cleaning up after them was degrading.

We used to have to wash their handkerchiefs and underwear by hand, a job that to this day has made me feel lower as a person than anything else.

To make it worse, every now and then Miss Boyle would appear and bitch at us for not working well, or hard enough, or in the right way. Miss Boyle loved an eye roll, loved to cluck her tongue – which was unable to fit around an R.

'Niamh,' she asked one day, 'why aren't these dishes washed yet?'

'I'm just going to hoover the—' Niamh began.

'Hoover?' Miss Boyle rolled her eyes. 'Surely you mean *vacuum?*'

I flinched when she said that. I would have used the word *hoover* too; everyone I knew did.

'*Hoover* is a brand,' Miss Boyle pontificated through a pursed mouth. 'The act is *to vacuum*. Please be sure to speak well or you will get nowhere in life. You don't want to be seen as "muck savages" your *whole* lives, do you?'

Sharon went 'Ehhh,' quite loudly in response to that, taking umbrage on all of our accounts. I wished she wouldn't. Whatever this was – this so-called course – *I* had left school for it.

I wanted to get the qualification. I wanted to get the distinction Miss O'Rourke had told me I could get. I'd just get through this for the papers.

Sharon needed to do the same.

'Well,' Miss Boyle said, then sniffed a few times as she lifted the item I was folding out of my hands and folded it in front of her in exactly the same way I had been. 'Come on, it's not rocket science,' she said.

'I was doing it—' I said, not even 16, sweating buckets running a college laundry.

'Ah ah,' she interrupted, 'imprudence is sinful.'

I had no idea what imprudence was. I had no idea what most of the words Miss Boyle used to describe us were. Except the insults she chose when she was really bored.

'A bunch of rotten apples,' she called us one time when we hadn't known to stir the sauce she had started for us and the bottom had burned out of the pan. There were four of us on in Gort Ard that week, standing there in the kitchen listening to her stinking out of her, her lips flapping and her pudgy hands pounding the table.

'Am I dealing with imbeciles? Idiots?' she asked us.

I smiled, tried to calm the onslaught. She looked at me in disgust.

'I have never known a girl with *such* a fake smile,' she announced. 'Is it a holiday you think you're on?'

Sharon, who I could see was getting angrier and angrier as the stink poured out of Miss Boyle, stamped her foot. 'No!' she said. 'We don't *think* it's a holiday! We *thought* it was a COURSE! But nobody has taught us nothing!'

We all nodded hard in agreement, and there was a brief moment where I thought Miss Boyle was coming to a realisation that there had been some mix-up. Her expression softened into a quizzical frown, as if she was realising she was here to teach, not direct.

But she just laughed out loud, and then went back to her office, leaving us to make the blancmange that was on the menu.

Mary Wilson was working up to something. I could see it on her face, she kept looking from girl to girl as we chatted.

'Oh yeah,' she said suddenly, as if she had just remembered to mention it, 'did any of ye notice Miss Diaz's shoulders at Mass this morning?'

I didn't say anything, but *I had*. I waited to see what others said.

'I did,' Sharon said, pleased to be in the know. '*That* was blood.'

Niamh gasped and I looked at her.

'I didn't see it,' she said, rubbing her wrist, 'maybe she hurt herself.'

'Yeah,' Mary Wilson said, and lowered her voice to a whisper, 'maybe she hurt *herself*.'

That confused me.

'Opus Dei are—' Mary went to continue.

'What are you rubbing your wrist for?' Sharon interrupted, speaking to Niamh. 'Have you still not found your watch?'

She hadn't.

'That's weird,' Mary Flanagan said. 'I can't find the stamps Mammy sent me last week.'

The conversation went that way, leaving Mary Wilson's observations for another time.

'I'm missing a stamp too,' Sharon said.

I caught Niamh's eye. Sharon Clark was not the tidiest girl we knew; it was no wonder she had mislaid a tiny scrap of paper. Her wardrobe was a total mess.

Miss Smith told us enough times that her wardrobe was a mirror to her soul. I wanted to keep mine clean and tidy in response to that.

'It says to add red colour,' Mary Wilson read from the sheet, and I ran to the baking press and retrieved a small bottle with a gold cap that said 'Red' on the front.

'This is it,' I said, coming back to Mary, and I unscrewed the top and poured a teaspoon of the liquid into the mix. As soon as Mary began to stir the milk I realised my mistake. The sauce, as it heated, became blood red, and no matter how much we stirred, it got brighter and brighter and brighter. I checked the recipe.

'Bloody hell,' I said, 'it says one drop, and I put a teaspoon.'

Niamh came over for a look and laughed out loud, and so did I, caught in the enjoyment of the mistake as the blancmange cooked and thickened. In the Grand we would have been on the floor over this, but we were too tired for hysterical giggles in Gort Ard.

'It looks like Marla,' Niamh said through giggles, thinking of the play dough every Irish child played with in school.

'I always loved Marla,' Sharon said, and let out a sigh. 'I tried to eat it a few times.'

'Well this one is edible, at least,' I said, and we all giggled.

But Miss Boyle didn't think so.

Her nose went up as soon as she saw the blancmange and the corners of her mouth went down. She came across the kitchen that way, miserable. 'Who made this?' she called out to the room, as if there were a hundred of us instead of four.

I raised my hand.

She lifted the dessert. I had turned it out from a mould onto a plate. A bright-red mountain of creamy jelly.

'Isn't it a bit loud?' she asked, and walked over and dumped it into the bin. 'Start again.'

She stood for a minute looking at us, one after the other. 'A pack of imbeciles,' she declared, and went back to her office.

Well, I was boiling. I wanted to scream after her that nobody was teaching us anything. But I kept it to myself.

The dessert came together just as it had before, but with the right colour. Making it against the clock made my skin feel like it was on fire and by the time it was done I felt like I couldn't breathe.

'What time is it?' Niamh still hadn't found her watch.

'Nearly eight o'clock,' Sharon said with a wince, 'and I haven't done the presses yet.'

'I'll help,' I said, and Niamh said she would too.

'No,' Sharon said, 'ye have enough to finish up yourselves – I'll do them now.'

We heard the green bus pull into the yard.

'Let me just finish these,' Sharon said, as we headed out of the kitchen to grab our stuff and go back to Ballyglunin. She sprayed and wiped as we normally did, and I stood waiting for her in the hallway. Then we left.

———

We returned the next morning, all exhausted, because as soon as we got back to Ballyglunin we'd had to help prepare the oratories for the next day and none of us got to bed until well after 10.30.

Before all of us were through the kitchen door Miss Boyle, who was already there, spun on her heel and shouted, 'What is this?'

Her hand slammed down on the counter. 'What is THIS?!'

She pulled the presses open and slammed them shut, all of them in a row. I looked around, and at first I had no idea what 'this' was.

But then I did.

The presses had been wiped hastily, and there were marks left by the cloth where the wet had dried in drips across the surface. It was something that would take less than two minutes to rectify.

But Miss Boyle loved to rant, and this was a great excuse. 'Who wiped these?!' she roared.

Sharon put her hand up. 'I didn't have much time—'

'How could you possibly do this?' Miss Boyle banged the press with her hand. 'This is disgraceful! What is this about? What are you thinking doing this?'

Sharon apologised and explained, and apologised and explained, until she was in tears and Miss Boyle was on a high, banging presses and looking for reasons to continue berating us.

She pulled the tarts we had made the day before from the fridge and poked the pastry.

'Dry!' she exclaimed. 'Who made these?'

We all looked at Sharon as she raised her hand.

'Oh, no surprises there!' Miss Boyle was red in the face with delight at that. She pulled out a tray of sandwiches and pulled at the cling film.

'Who wrapped these?' she said, and I put up my hand.

'Well,' Miss Boyle said, 'I would have been sure Sharon was the one who wrapped this, probably hoping to make them stale.'

'I can't take this!' Sharon's hands went over her ears and she started shaking. She clutched her head and ran from the room.

Miss Boyle opened every drawer and emptied them with her hands onto the floor.

'Sharon!' she called into the hall. 'Get back here and clean this mess up!'

I looked at Niamh with a hammering heart. This was mad. She looked at me the same way. What was happening?

Miss Boyle left the room and went into her little office. We went after Sharon and found her in a ball in the corner of the changing room, crying her eyes out.

'I'm so confused,' she said, as I sat down and put my arm around her.

'Come on back,' I said, and we stood up like that.

Niamh straightened her sleeves for her, running the tap and handing her a towel while Sharon washed her face.

'Get a towel,' I told Niamh, and she slipped out to get one from the laundry.

'We are supposed to be training,' Sharon said. 'Nobody is teaching us anything, we are just slaving away for nothing, and we have all left school for this crap.'

'Look,' Niamh said, coming back through the door, 'we will get our diploma either way, and maybe learning on the job is tried and tested.'

'You just want to think that, Niamh,' Sharon snapped, 'because it's your fault we are all here.'

'Hey!' I put my hand up. 'That's ridiculous. Niamh didn't make you come. You did that yourself.'

Sharon bit her tongue then. But I could see the impact her words had had on Niamh. Her face was white, as if her own inner thoughts were being exposed.

'Why don't you leave if you hate it?' she asked.

'I left school for this shit.' Sharon put it right to her with a finger in her face, and then she looked at me with just as much venom as she had for Niamh and shoved my hand off her arm. She left the room.

When we went back into the kitchen Sharon was replacing the kitchen tools into the drawer as we had been told to do it, arranging them by size. So I took up a spray and a sponge and set about cleaning the presses.

Eleven

'Are you going to Mass?' Niamh asked me, and I nodded. We had been in Ballyglunin for six months.

She looked around her. 'I know it's been ages but I still keep thinking I might find my watch,' she said, showing me her empty wrist. 'I've no idea where it went to.'

She pulled at drawers and looked in the kitchen presses.

'I don't know, Niamh, it seems to be gone,' I said, but I looked in drawers and presses too.

'Mass is on now,' Mary Wilson said, leaning on the door frame.

Sharon came in, and she did not look ready at all. She mooched around, taking some cereal into a bowl.

'Mass is on now,' I said.

'Oh right,' she said, and ate a spoonful of cereal. 'I'm not going.'

'What will I tell them?' I asked, worried.

'They won't notice,' she said. 'They're too busy whipping themselves to give a shit about us.'

I snapped my head around.

'They do not do that,' I said, and Sharon put her hands on her hips.

'They absolutely do,' she said. 'They practically told us about it one of the days you were over beyond, and I heard

Miss O'Rourke at it last Saturday when I was passing the bathroom, yelping and all, she was.'

'You didn't,' I said, but I knew she must have, because I had too. In the dark of the nighttime passing the bathroom you often heard someone lashing themselves and praying really fast. But even if I hadn't, I knew Sharon was brave and brave people didn't need to lie.

Niamh looked for her watch fruitlessly again, and we made Mass with a minute to go, slipping in at the back and rushing to our usual spot. The other girls slid across the seat to make way for us to sit down.

'Do you know what Miss O'Rourke told me this morning?' Mary Wilson whispered, and leaned in so the two of us could hear, lowering her voice right down. 'Standing outside there,' she nodded to the door, 'waiting for Mass, she said to me that if you say bad things about Opus Dei ... like if you talked dirt about them, let's say, she said terrible things will then happen to you.'

'Why did she say that?' I said.

Mary Wilson shrugged, but went on: 'The only thing I can think is that I was on the phone to my dad last night – look I was saying one thing, that it's a bit weird and intense here, and I saw she was over by the doorway so I stopped talking. Anyway she took me aside this morning and told me what I said there, random like, and then,' Mary looked around because the priest was coming and so we stood up, 'then ... she told me about a little boy in Dublin ... who ended up getting ...' Mary's face went white, 'actually crucified to the floor of his house, in the attic, because his parents were in Opus Dei.'

'*Crucified?*' I couldn't believe she meant that word. 'Like Jesus?'

Miss Smith turned and shot us daggers with her eyes for talking.

'Apparently.' Mary Wilson shrugged again.

I decided in that moment that Mary was making that up, trying to make me believe it as some kind of prank, and so I didn't really talk to Mary Wilson that day. I stayed away from her. The story was so unsettling either way, I didn't want to be near it.

———

'Good morning, girls.' The teachers passed us as we got ready to serve breakfast in their dining room. That morning we had orange juice, boiled eggs and toast, and pots of tea and coffee – real coffee for them and chicory coffee for us.

We served the food to them and Miss O'Rourke said, 'Thank you.' Immediately, that felt throwaway.

Miss Diaz lifted her eyes as I put down a basket of boiled eggs lined with a linen napkin in the centre of the table. She took an egg and with a small silver spoon, and topped the egg open, revealing a hard-boiled yolk. She shook her head and sighed heavily.

'Can you remove the glasses, girls, please?' Miss O'Rourke said as we went to leave the dining room, so we collected them up and went out the door. It wasn't easy to close the door with the glasses in our hands, and it didn't click and bounced open a little in the frame, so I turned to close it properly.

'Dear me, they can't even boil an egg,' I overheard Miss Diaz say.

I went down the stairs again with burning cheeks and said nothing. But inside I was boiling myself.

This pressure cooker of an existence felt as if it was making me sick. My stomach felt knotted, and it was as if there was an actual physical weight on my shoulders. I could see the others felt that way too. We were all living this, learning nothing but expected to cook elaborate meals. Their lunch and dinner choices left in plastic sleeves along with the to-do list that we would find on the counter each day.

I spent my days cleaning, imagining myself taking these women to task, imagining myself jumping across the table and demanding answers. My mouth would move with my internal arguments; the debates that would swirl around in my head came out in my dreams and I would wake breathless, having screamed myself blue in my subconscious.

Sometimes in my imagination I would shake them and slap their faces.

———

One day, a batch of mince pies were just out of the oven, cooling, and everything was fine, when Miss Boyle came in. She stared at the pies, and it seemed there was no problem, so she moved on, swiping her finger along the countertop and opening random drawers. She checked the sink and even smelled the sponges. There was nothing to pick on.

She rounded back on me. I was scraping the bits I had collected from the countertop onto a plastic chopping board, about to cross to the bin. She stopped me.

'What's this?' she asked, pressing a finger into the ends of pastry gathered in a ball on the side.

'Oh,' I said, 'it's from the pies.' I lifted the board in the direction of my lovely mince pies, with their decorations, which were still bubbling away from the heat of the oven, placed on the ledge to cool. I was proud of them.

She looked at them and then back to the board.

'What's that?' she asked again, peering with an eagle eye into one of the bowls.

I looked and didn't see anything.

She poked and pulled with her nail and I saw the end of a garlic clove, the little hard bit that you slice off, stuck to her fingertip.

'Oh,' I said and removed it for her, 'I scraped the counter in the bowl after.'

'Garlic,' she said, and she looked down her nose at it.

Then she turned. 'Mary!' Mary Flanagan turned around and Miss Boyle pointed at the mince pies. 'Bin these, please, and would you mind doing a fresh batch? Thank you. Such a waste of good ingredients that cost money.'

Halfway through her sentence I realised what she was saying. The mince pies I had worked so hard on were, in her view, contaminated by a tiny thing that had probably just fallen off my knife or my hand when I pushed all the scraps in from the pastry board.

'No!' I shouted at Mary Flanagan. 'There is nothing wrong with them – leave them alone.'

I crossed the kitchen, waving my hand. Mary stood still.

'The pies are fine,' I said. 'It was just on the counter – I didn't make them on this board anyway.'

The garlic scrap, though I had no idea where it came from, had gone nowhere near the pies. It was Miss Boyle's excuse to torture me. I hadn't given her any in a few weeks and she was hungry for it.

'We will not serve contaminated food,' she said after me. And then she pushed past me with her huge tummy, lifted the pies herself and binned them.

As they slid off the trays into the bin, those little perfect pies with their holly cut-outs, the frustration inside me exploded like a bomb.

'You're a BITCH!' I cried out as Miss Boyle walked out of the room in her usual way. She didn't miss a step and closed the door behind her. I raced across the kitchen to open the door and shout again, but Mary Wilson barred my way.

'Stop, stay away from her,' she said. 'Feck her, Anne Marie, don't rise to it.'

'I will punch her fat face!' I screamed at the door. 'You fucking BITCH!'

Mary Donovan held me back too. 'Anne Marie, don't, don't!'

I wrestled with them, freeing my arms, pushing and taking a step forward against their weight, finally making it to the door and pulling it, but Mary Donovan shoved her bum into it, closing it again.

'Stop!' she shouted at me. 'Take a breath.'

'This isn't learning! We are supposed to be learning!' I shouted, and burst into tears.

I was so disappointed, in that moment, that we were there slaving all day and learning nothing, unless we taught ourselves, that as I slid to the floor on my hunkers, I began to cry my eyes out.

I was just so bitterly disappointed.

———

We decided to complain. Mary Wilson said she would speak, and I would back her up. The rest of the girls, or at least some of us, would stand in solidarity with one another. We were going to form a little union.

Mary Donovan had disagreed. 'They aren't going to change anything; they probably won't even listen,' she said. 'They're all for each other, them lot, and they'll be for Miss Boyle. Opus Dei are like that – they are only loyal to Opus Dei.'

Once she said that, one or two other girls stepped back from the complaining party.

'I really do believe Miss O'Rourke and Miss Smith care,' Niamh said. 'They have to listen – we are supposed to be doing a course. There's been a mistake.'

'All of us have been lied to,' Sharon said, 'by Miss O'Rourke and Miss Smith. Sorry, Niamh, but we have to stand up for ourselves.'

'Fine then,' Niamh said, 'I just …' She didn't finish her sentence and I felt really sorry for her then. I knew she was feeling like this was all her fault.

'I'll ask for a meeting,' I said. 'These are holy women. Niamh is right, they do care, and they will be so angry when they hear this.'

But I wasn't sure.

———

'Ah!' Miss O'Rourke said when I came in the door. 'Lovely Anne Marie, are you looking for me?'

I was; I had called her name a few times on my way up the stairs. Miss O'Rourke moved up on the couch and patted it for me to sit beside her.

'We need to speak to you, Miss O'Rourke,' I said as I sat down. 'All of us do. We are unhappy.'

She seemed less than enthusiastic as soon as I said that. I noticed a real change in the energy in the room, but even so, she didn't ask what the meeting was for. She just smiled and took a deep breath and held it. Then she said, 'Sure, sure, come see me after everything is done this evening, in my bedroom.'

'What does the Bible say about slavery?' Sharon asked the numeraries that evening as she was laying the table for dinner. 'I'm codding, I'm codding,' she added, and Miss Smith gave a tight smile.

Miss O'Rourke looked furious. I hurried placing the food down. I wanted to get us out of there before Sharon got us in trouble.

'What are your plans after graduating, Anne Marie?' Miss O'Reilly asked suddenly, as Sharon went ahead of me out of the room. She didn't stop but I did. I turned around and said I wanted a job in a hotel maybe, but really I didn't know yet.

The three directors smiled at each other.

'What?' I asked, wondering if I had said something wrong.

Miss O'Reilly looked smug. 'I think *we* know what you want to do,' she said.

I stared at them, feeling out of the loop.

'Doesn't it seem like this house is like a real home to you?' Miss Smith asked, and the other numeraries stifled soft giggles.

I smiled, tried to look like I was in on the joke. But as I went to the kitchen, running after Sharon, I didn't know at all what they meant by any of that.

————

We piled into Miss O'Rourke's bedroom as soon as we saw her go in after supper. We told her everything, all about how we weren't learning anything, that we were desperate and upset.

'And being really bullied down in Gort Ard by Miss Boyle,' I added.

'She is the worst,' Sharon said.

Mary Donovan piped up too. 'She is so awful to us.'

Miss O'Rourke give a little smile, I thought, but then she flashed her eyes and flared her nostrils as if she was hearing something really obnoxious.

I stuttered as I tried to speak more. 'W-we-we—'

Sharon took over. 'We signed up to do a course, Miss O'Rourke, and we haven't learned nothing!'

'We've really learned nothing,' Mary Wilson agreed, 'and Miss Boyle is bullying us! She tells us to do what we don't know how to do, and then kills us for getting it wrong.'

We became a chorus, all complaining at once, all speaking over each other. Listing off on our fingers the wrongs we had been done.

Finally we were quiet.

Miss O'Rourke slid her gaze from girl to girl. Then she spoke.

'I have listened to you; now, girls, please listen to me.' She stood and went to the door. 'Miss Boyle is a good honest member of the Work; she is a member of this Opus Dei family, both on a small scale and a large one,' she said through a pursed mouth. 'I will not have her spoken about like this. Maybe the fault is with you. If you leave now you will have no Leaving Cert, no qualifications, and will not be able to get a job. It seems to me that you need to get on with it and stop complaining.'

Miss O'Rourke opened the door and pointed for us to leave. I stared at her and for a moment she stared back, then dropped her eyes from my head to my toes with a disgusted look. I felt the impact of that look through me.

We filed out and she shut the door behind us.

Sharon Clark mouthed the words 'What the hell?' at me but I didn't know what to say in response. I was stunned.

'What do we do now?' Niamh asked.

'We get on with it,' Mary Donovan said, pushing past us and down the stairs. 'We are already behind now with this silliness. I told you they don't give a shit, I told you it would make no difference. Let's get to the end of it and get our diplomas.'

We followed her down the stairs and into the kitchen, because she was right.

Sharon Clark turned on us for answers that she couldn't find herself as soon as we got back into the kitchen. 'What are we getting out of this?'

I shrugged and opened the fridge. There was a cake on the list for tomorrow and I wanted to see what they had provided me to make it with. So many times the ingredients on the recipe would be nowhere to be found.

Niamh spoke up. 'I think it's a new style of learning,' she said.

'Oh here we go,' Mary Donovan said. 'New learning, did you say? How would you figure that one now?'

'Well ...' Niamh held her breath for a pause, 'we are doing a kind of learn-on-the-job thing, getting experience while we go.'

'Getting experience in what? Slavery?' Sharon retorted, banging on the overhead light and rinsing a cloth to wipe down the counters. 'Experience in getting in trouble for getting things wrong when not one of them taught us one minute of anything?'

Niamh burst out crying.

'Oh shut up crying!' Sharon said. Her hands rested on her hips and she stared at Niamh. 'I cannot believe you convinced me to come here!'

I said nothing. Inside of my head I was so frustrated I almost wanted to join in and turn on Niamh, but I didn't, because I knew it wasn't her fault. It really wasn't. This wasn't what we thought it was going to be. But it was no reason to attack each other.

'And why,' Sharon said, 'did they ask us to bring all the things they told us? Why do I have togs with me?'

'I don't even need my coat,' said Mary Donovan. 'All I go to is Gort Ard – I thought there would be days off and excursions.'

'I wouldn't care about that if I was learning something,' Sharon said, and gave Niamh a dirty look. 'And I wasn't going to bring this up, but someone is stealing stuff. Mary has lost her fiver, and my white socks are gone.'

Mary Donovan nodded. Niamh grabbed her wrist where her watch was missing and her mouth went into an O. Mine did too. I think it had crossed all our minds. But it was a big accusation all the same.

Sharon started flicking through cookery books. 'I tell you I won't go to Mass seven days a week with these lunatics,' she said. 'I won't be going again till Sunday.'

'Let's all not go,' Mary Flanagan said, 'like a protest.'

Twelve

'Miss O'Rourke told me Sharon Clark is complaining again,' Miss Smith said. We were on our weekly tutoring session, walking around the grounds. These sessions were not about tutoring, which was confusing. They were these strange counselling talks – nothing to do with study – where you'd be asked question after question about your life and thoughts.

I was stilled by that announcement about Sharon: it wasn't just her complaining, it was all of us. We were all miserable.

Miss Smith exhaled loudly, and squeezed my arm. 'And it didn't go unnoticed that none of you were in Mass the last few mornings.' She looked meek and upset.

I inhaled as if to speak, but then I closed my mouth.

'We should all love the Sacrament of the Eucharist deeply,' Miss Smith said, and she nodded to herself and pressed her hand against her heart. Then she stopped walking and turned to me. 'Anne Marie, some girls are always looking for the negative in life,' she said. 'Thank God you are not like that.'

My thoughts shifted inside my head, one step to the right. Was I different? I couldn't see how. I had complained along with everyone – I had kind of led the charge, in fact. But they didn't see that, and it felt confusing, but ... it felt good to be favoured. I was never favoured by anyone.

'I think they were hoping to go swimming,' I said, and it was nothing to do with anything, but it was something to say.

'Were they?' Miss Smith asked, and I hated the *they* because it was a *we*, and I should have said *we*.

But I nodded anyway.

'You know, I have to say, Anne Marie,' she said, 'you are someone I have an awful lot of time for. You're such a virtuous, intelligent and popular young woman. Sometimes I forget you aren't one of us.'

I liked to hear those things. Miss Smith really was so together and so cool, and she always looked so beautiful.

'I worry about you, though.' She whispered it, folding her arms as if she was cold.

'Why?' I asked, my mind racing.

'Well,' she said, 'I know things are hard at home.' She lingered over the sentence, to let the inference settle. 'I know your mother suffers with ...' She didn't finish the line.

I was instantly embarrassed, right down to my toes.

'Honestly, Anne Marie,' she went on, 'I know you worry a lot about it.' I did not how she knew about that.

'You should pray for your mother. You should go to the oratory and pray every day. Things will really improve for her if you pray,' Miss Smith said.

How did she know? It felt like she could really see who I felt I was, and what life I was dealing with.

'Are you happy here?' she asked me. 'I know the other girls are being difficult, but I said to Miss Diaz and Miss Byrne at dinner that I just knew that you were happy. I could sense it.'

I didn't want to disrupt the warmth, so I nodded and said I was.

'Do you promise?' she asked, seeming giddy and childish all of a sudden.

I promised.

'I knew it!' She seemed really happy. Then she sighed. 'I worry, though, Sharon Clark is the kind of girl that will never do well anywhere – too spoiled. Isn't she?'

I said yes.

'I'll tell you something, but you cannot tell the girls,' Miss Smith said. 'The reason we can't go swimming is because that time when we were thinking of going we realised … well, Sharon Clark has a … bikini … and … well, girls wearing those is sinful, and we cannot be seen to …' Her voice trailed off.

I was surprised that Miss Smith was saying this to me. I shared a room with Sharon. And anyway, most girls had bikinis.

'I mean look, Sharon isn't a bad person,' Miss Smith said, 'or at least she probably doesn't intend to be, but' – she squeezed my arm – 'you are more the kind of girl that suits Ballyglunin, you know? It's like you're one of us. Miss O'Rourke says so too. And Miss Diaz said it the other day.'

I still loved praise. I thrived on it. None of the other girls, not even Niamh, gave me confidence boosts the way Miss Smith and Miss O'Rourke did when they told me I was more like them. They were so beautiful, clever and together. They reminded me of Aunt Bernadette, devoted to Our Lord, and they seemed to make other people become calm and considered.

'Miss Diaz said so?' I wanted to hear about that. Miss Diaz frightened me but I still wanted her approval.

'Oh, would you stop?' Miss Smith said, giggling. 'Miss Diaz thinks you are amazing – she told me she thinks you'll be running the course next year.'

I giggled as well, the same way as she had. But inside of my head I knew you could not be a teacher without a Leaving. I lied to myself anyway, told myself she knew more than anyone about these things.

'Maybe you could ask Sharon to go to the oratory with you, and maybe go to Mass as well,' Miss Smith advised then, 'and hope she sees that Opus Dei want to help her in her life, because that is the truth. And you know, Anne Marie, people who turn against Opus Dei do not have happy lives.'

I wasn't sure what to say.

She continued, 'I have seen that when someone speaks badly about Opus Dei it is only a matter of time until something terrible happens to them.'

'Can I ask you something?' I said. Miss Smith slowed down. 'Mary told me this thing, about a boy in Dublin ... she said he was ... crucified.'

Miss Smith's hand flew to her mouth. She stopped in her tracks and without looking at me she said, 'Yes, it's true.'

My mind was blown. 'Really?' I started to chatter. 'Crucified? Like on a cross? Are you serious, Miss Smith? What did the family do? How did anyone do that? Was it Opus Dei that done it?'

'Sssh!' she said. 'Stop this!'

I shut up.

'The Devil does not like Opus Dei, Anne Marie,' she said, wagging a finger at me, 'because we do so much good in the world.'

I kept my eyes on hers. This was true?

'"You must live by your own heart,"' Miss Smith started to quote to me as we headed back to the house. '"Let your 'Yes' mean 'Yes', and your 'No' mean 'No'. Anything more is from the evil one." Now isn't that a beautiful quote?'

I nodded, even though I had no idea what it meant. She must have sensed that, because she continued, 'It means that people are easily influenced to go in with the Devil, so you have to watch who you're in with.'

The air around me went cold. I wanted to go back inside.

'I think if you really pray to the guardian angels, Anne Marie,' Miss Smith said as she led me back, 'and give yourself up to God, every day, all day, through doing the little things, this world will get better for you. And for your family. If you turn against God, or against Opus Dei, God will punish you.'

It felt like that could be true. But I couldn't figure out if it was God or the Devil I should be scared of.

A week later Sharon Clark got word that her mother had died. As we sat in the recreation room for our get-together I could hear the sounds of her wails from the hallways.

And I was absolutely terrified.

———

'Do you think it's because she was saying all that stuff?' I whispered to Mary Wilson when Sharon left for the funeral. We were sitting on my bed, sorting out our socks into pairs.

'Saying what, like?' Mary asked me.

'Saying bad things about Opus Dei,' I said, 'you know …
like the boy in Dublin did?'

Mary moved back sharply and shook her head, as if the idea
was a wasp.

'I don't think so, Anne Marie,' she said, sounding wiser
than me, 'and anyway that crucified boy story makes no sense
– his parents were *in* Opus Dei.'

I didn't see her point.

'Why would they be harmed,' she pointed out, 'if being in
Opus Dei is what God wants you to do?'

I didn't know how to make the ends of this idea meet. 'Well,
Miss Smith said the Devil hates Opus Dei.'

'I don't see how,' Mary said, and threw the balled socks in
her hands up into the air and caught them again, 'and they
don't seem to either, to be honest.'

I didn't know how to see *how* either; my mind wasn't able
to follow their explanations.

'They're full of crap, Anne Marie,' Mary said. I wished she
wouldn't, and I decided not to talk to her about it just in case
God thought I agreed with her.

The next time I went to meet Miss Smith for our one-to-
one, I asked her again if punishment was something that really
happened.

'Yes, Anne Marie,' she said firmly, 'when you speak out
against Opus Dei or commit a mortal sin, God finds a way to
punish you. It's true – think about that child in Dublin.'

I took the opportunity. 'But … if his parents were in Opus
Dei, why were they being punished?'

'How do you mean?' Miss Smith kept her tone so friendly.

'Well, Mary Wilson was saying that they were in Opus Dei,' I said, 'and their child was the one who was killed ... so ... it's just ... what did God get angry for?'

Miss Smith was sitting at her little desk and I was sitting on her bed. She had been facing me, but she shifted herself in the seat when I said that, and leaned away from me. 'Anne Marie,' she said, 'are crucified children a joke among you and your pals across?' Her eyes flashed as she spoke. She looked furious.

I didn't understand the question. I thought about what I had said: I hadn't made a joke at all. I stuttered something.

Then, like a cloud passing, she calmed and reverted to her friendly self, and I was relieved and wondered had I imagined the change. She leaned forward, holding onto her own hands, and said, 'You're the cleverest girl here. If the rest aren't understanding what we are about, it's not our fault, is it?'

I sat up a bit straighter. I thought about Niamh and how clever she was, and how much fun I would have with Sharon when we were doing the laundry and she would egg me on to switch the bras of the teachers in their laundry bags, and I thought about the three Marys and how they'd get the giggles together when we did that, and how much I liked all of them.

'Just ignore them,' Miss Smith said.

'Oh, but ... I don't mean that ... I ... everyone is really nice in the class, they're not being bad, and I was saying it as well.' I felt relief speaking like that. I loved the feeling of truth: it filled my lungs like good air, and made me feel really strong.

'Ah.' Miss Smith nodded, still smiling. 'I understand ...' Then she looked confused. 'I think!'

———

When my mam rang later, on the phone in the basement hall between the kitchen and main house, I told her what Miss Smith had said about becoming a teacher.

My mam seemed quiet and distracted. I hoped she wasn't feeling bad again.

My dad's voice came down the line. 'Sure that's grand now.' I realised he was listening in to the same receiver.

My mother sighed. 'I told you this course was the ticket for Anne Marie,' she said.

My dad grumbled a little and then he laughed. 'You did, Peg, you did.'

'How are the lectures?' my aunt Bernadette asked later, on another call. Miss O'Rourke was standing a few feet away, looking like she was waiting to use the phone.

'Great!' I lied. 'I'm learning so much.'

'What did you learn today?' Bernadette wasn't suspicious, it was a normal question, but I felt an edge.

'All about food hygiene,' I said, and told her there were people waiting on the phone so I had to go. Then I went upstairs to where all the other girls were waiting for the get-together in the recreation room.

'Where were you?' Mary Wilson asked.

'Nowhere you mind,' I snapped, and she was surprised by it, but I didn't care. I just sat down beside Niamh and slumped back with my arms folded, looking straight ahead at no one. Whatever was going on, I was going to finish this course and get the qualification and the job. I'd show Bernadette and the others and anyone who didn't think this was a course. Maybe I would never go home, and people would never see me again. That would teach them with their questions.

'Has anyone seen my little brown notebook?' Mary Flanagan asked around, but we all shook our heads. 'That's another thing missing,' she said, and stared at me. I looked away. I was missing stamps myself. I just hadn't brought it up because I was not in the mood for another conversation about how crap this course was.

―――――

We were in the kitchen when Miss O'Rourke came in. She came down with Mary Flanagan just ahead of her, and she took the two last steps as one and scuttled in past us all to the back of the kitchen. That was unusual: Mary Flanagan usually went straight to her room when the work was all over, while the rest of us hung around.

'Anne Marie – a word, please,' said Miss O'Rourke. There was no smile.

I rinsed and dried my hands and ran after her as she was already heading off, out of the building toward the cold food storage tower in the mews.

When I caught up, she was gathering some dry ingredients and was not looking at me. She seemed off, with her mouth twisted and saying nothing. It scared me, and the cold of that room got to me until I ended up shivering so much my teeth chattered. Then she turned.

'We think that it is you who might be doing the stealing,' she said finally.

It took me a second or two to register the words and my heartbeat suddenly took over my head, banging in my ears as my stomach plummeted.

'What?' I couldn't say anything else but that.

'Things have been going missing; every single girl has reported that to their tutor,' Miss O'Rourke said.

'I lost stamps,' I said, and my hands flew out in defence. 'I lost my stamps, five stamps … I lost—'

'We know it's you, Anne Marie,' she said, 'and we are currently investigating, and if we find proof you will be expelled, sent home, and you'll never ever get a job. You will be sent home in shame to your village, believe me.'

I shook my head sincerely, pleading. 'You can search my things, you can look …'

She stared at me for a moment. The pause felt like forever.

Then she put a hand on her pocket. 'Father Gannon got a letter from your parish priest,' she said, patting it again as if the letter was in there, 'telling us here that you are a known thief in Ballyvourney.'

The words were nonsense and a lie. I knew they had to be. I'd never stolen anything. But even so, panic spiralled in my body. I wanted to strangle her, or run from her, to stop her saying such terrible things that I couldn't believe. I had never in my life stolen one thing.

'It's not true,' I said, and I couldn't stand there. The adrenaline that was pumping through me was so uncomfortable I just had to get away from her. 'It is not true!' I shouted, and turned and ran as fast as I could back to the house.

Mary Donovan was in the bedroom when I flew in, coming from her own room to bunk in with us while Sharon was away. 'Girls can't be left in twos,' she had repeated, mocking Miss O'Rourke, as she dragged her case across the floor from room to room. 'God only knows what kinds of things ye'd be getting up to.'

Now, she looked up in surprise as I came through the door and closed it behind me, breathing like I had been in a fight. 'Jesus, girl,' she said. She looked so pale and tired.

'Miss O'Rourke just … accused me … of stealing from everyone,' I said.

Her eyebrows shot up. 'Ah Jesus, that's crazy,' she said, but then she stopped what she was doing and added, 'or is it you?'

I shook my head adamantly, catching my breath. 'Of course not,' I said, and I told her the whole story.

'Did she say that?' she asked then, narrowing her eyes and flattening her mouth into a hard line. 'Find Father Gannon on Wednesday. He will be here to do Confession – you can ask him.'

———

I watched the window all Wednesday morning for Father Gannon's car and I was first in line for Confession when he finally arrived. I barely slept with the anticipation of finding out who had written to him with such abominable lies. I had to ask him, because I knew it couldn't be our parish priest, because he wouldn't lie like that. There must be some mistake in the letter. I needed to know.

'Hello, Anne Marie,' Father Gannon said. It was surprising that he remembered my name since none of us had been going to Mass or Confession at all the last few weeks, except for on Sundays.

I could not wait to ask him straight out. 'Father, did you get a letter about me from my parish priest?'

His eyebrows fused together in a frown. 'I did,' he confirmed.

'What did the letter say about me?'

'Well,' he said, 'let me remember how it was put now, eh … so … right, yes … it said, "Anne Marie is a sweet local girl that comes from a good family and that I hope would be well looked after in the school."'

'Did he say anything else?' I asked him, holding myself back from clutching his lapel and shaking him.

'No, he just said that. Are you all right, Anne Marie?'

I knew I must be red in the face; I could feel it. 'I'm fine, Father,' I said. 'I am sorry for asking.'

'Would you like me to hear your confession?' he asked. I nodded and made the Sign of the Cross.

'Bless me, Father, for I have sinned,' I said. 'It has been a week since my last confession.'

Thirteen

I wanted to go to Rome but I didn't have the money and my dad wasn't able to send it.

'We just don't have it, love,' he said when I asked.

'I can't go,' I said to Miss Smith.

She shook her head and told me not to be negative. At the get-together that night, she brought it up and asked people how we could get the money to get me to Rome.

'Nobody deserves this trip more than Anne Marie,' she said, and a few of my classmates rolled their eyes.

'We could do a bake sale outside the local church,' Mary Flanagan said. She was going to Rome, all paid up already.

So we set up tables in front of the local church and we sold cream cakes, sponge cakes and buns over two Sundays to the local people.

Miss Smith loved counting the money collected. 'We will get you there,' she kept saying, licking her fingers and thumbing through the notes, before tucking them into an envelope that had my name on it.

'God will not leave you behind us,' Miss Diaz said.

Then we held a sponsored cycle to Tuam and back.

They could not stop speaking about this fundraiser at every get-together. It felt like all eyes were on me – the poor girl.

Even in the community, it seemed that people were looking down on me as they gave five pence or a penny to my cause.

But before the month was out I had a ticket to Rome with my name on. All I needed was a passport. When the post office announced a strike, we realised we wouldn't get the passport posted back to us on time, and so four of us were bundled into the train and directed to the Molesworth Street passport office with the four photos I'd had taken in the train station in Galway that morning.

'What is the craic with you?' Mary Donovan said as we took our seats in the train on the way back to Tuam. 'It's not just Rome, sure it's not? You're joining them, aren't you?'

I said nothing. Mary never usually spoke to me like this. Niamh was looking at me from her seat, listening in.

'You used to be one of us,' Mary went on. 'Now you're like a lost lamb, following the holies around.'

I didn't answer.

'Are you joining Opus Dei?' Niamh asked.

'Why do ye care so much?' I said, folding my arms and slumping in my seat.

'We had a plan to be chefs together,' Niamh said. 'That's why I care.'

'No,' I told her, '*I* had a plan – to go to London. You wanted to tag along. Just get your own life, Niamh, and leave me alone.'

Niamh shut up. Mary Donovan looked out the window.

I picked the skin of my elbows until it stung.

———

Just before we went to Rome, a few of us, me, Niamh and Mary Flanagan, were signed up to go to a talk in the catering college in Dartry, Dublin. It was last minute. Miss Smith drove us all the way there in the green bus.

'Anne Marie is going to sit here,' she said, putting her hand on the pad of the front seat as soon as Mary Flanagan opened the van door. I was chuffed with that. Mary Flanagan did a little curtsy as I took the place and I just stared out the window as she clambered into the back. I knew she preferred that seat because she was so tall. She had gone in the front since day one.

Miss Smith chatted straight to me all the way, talking about how wonderful Rome would be and how much fun we could have. She told me about the girls we were going to meet.

I could feel Mary Flanagan's knees digging into the back of my seat all the way.

In Dartry, we met a group of catering students just like us, only there were three times as many in that place. Their uniforms were spotless as well, and ours were still so stained. I spent the day trying to hide somehow, pulling my cardigan down over my knees when we sat down and wrapping it around me when I was standing.

We stood in small groups and swapped information. They had a domestic science teacher coming in to them at least once or twice a week, the girl closest to me said.

'I'm Catherine,' she said suddenly, sticking her hand out, and shaking mine and Niamh's. 'Doyle.'

I knew that name. Miss Smith had been talking about Catherine in the car. Catherine was a year ahead of me in the course, she told me, and a full member of Opus Dei too.

'Are you Anne Marie?' she asked. 'You're coming to Rome, aren't you? So am I! Come, let me show you around.'

Niamh took a tiny step back just as I took a step forward, and Catherine and I walked off. Catherine never even asked Niamh to come with us and because I was going to Rome, it felt right to walk away. I'd need a friend over there, I told myself.

I noticed Catherine slow up as she entered each room ahead of me, and she looked up piously at the crucifix with a little nod. I copied her.

She showed me around – and for the whole time it was just the two of us – we talked about Rome, and I just agreed with everything and laughed when she did. Half of what she said was hard to follow. She spoke in quotes that felt like riddles.

'"For as long as you delay the decision to serve, your dealings with your brothers, colleagues and friends will be a constant source of disappointment",' Catherine recited. 'Have you heard that quote, Anne Marie?'

I said I hadn't. It was gobbledegook to me.

'I'm an assistant numerary,' Catherine said as we got to the dining hall, 'and I love my life now so much.'

I nodded, taking the seat she pulled out for me.

'Would you consider whistling yourself?' she asked me. I knew what she meant: 'whistling' was what Opus Dei called joining the organisation.

I said I didn't know.

'Before I always felt like I didn't know,' she told me. 'I always felt like I was on the outside of everything. Like I didn't know what I was doing … or something … it's hard to remember, because I don't feel that now. Now I feel like I know exactly what my life is for.'

I wished I did.

———

I went to Confession. We all did; it was routine and part and parcel of Ballyglunin life. Filing in to tell the priest all your secrets, a scam to keep us all under the thumb. We were as innocent as Irish country girls could be, but we still *felt* guilty.

I used to talk to Father Thorton, who came from Gort Ard to Ballyglunin Park to hear the human thoughts of teenage girls presented to him as if they were crimes.

'I had bad thoughts, Father,' I said this one time, and heard the priest sigh.

'I understand,' Father Thorton said, 'but you must not let these thoughts invade the purity of your soul.'

I said a prayer with him and he gave me some penance to do.

As I stood to leave he pulled back the little door between us. 'I hear you are thinking about joining Opus Dei.'

I wasn't really thinking that, but I didn't want to be rude. Not to a priest. So I nodded my head.

'Maybe God is calling you to be an assistant numerary,' he said.

———

The flight to Rome was my first. I stewed for the whole thing, replaying my faux pas with the air hostess: she had served us a drink of orange and I had downed mine before she had even poured one for the passenger to my left. I'd asked for another and been given a disapproving frown instead.

'That's very cheeky,' she said, and ignored my request. I spent the rest of the flight fighting with my humiliation. It won.

'You're sharing with me,' a woman called Anna said, patting me on the arm as we arrived at our bedroom. She was an assistant numerary, she said, one of the longest-serving assistant numeraries in Ireland.

'It's a wonderful life,' she told me.

I was a little disappointed to see Mary Flanagan was sharing with us too. She was sitting on the bed as we came in. But I remembered: only three or five to a bedroom, no pairs.

On our way back down a young woman – barely in her thirties – caught up with us and introduced herself as Miss Moloney.

'But you can call me Susan,' she said. I liked her immediately. She was warm, the kind of woman who walked really close as you went along, and it was comforting how much she seemed to take to me. She nodded constantly even when nobody was speaking.

'You're a super person,' she told me. 'I have heard great things about you.'

I asked Susan why we did not have to call her *Miss* like all of the directors. She said she had a different 'calling' and it would be fine to call her Susan.

'Opus Dei is a family,' she said. 'We are all sisters, all the same. I am an assistant numerary like Anna,' she explained, 'so *we* can call each other by our first names.'

I was a bit confused.

Rome was exactly like I'd imagined. I'd never heard noise like it, the constant beep-beep of tiny cars, loud chat from the locals on the streets, and the constant, humming to-ing and fro-ing of everyone and everything.

'I think,' Susan said, as we attempted to have a conversation while walking almost single file on a tiny footpath that evening, 'you should write a letter to Álvaro del Portillo, the Father, tomorrow and see if you could get admission as a member … just as a formality before you decide.'

The way she said *could*, it was as if it was something exclusive.

I wondered who had told her about this idea. I had only ever met her briefly before and I had never shared any information with her.

'I knew a guy before,' Susan said, 'he had a vocation just like you do, a huge one, but he refused to see it. He was stubborn, and, well …' Her face took on an exaggerated expression. 'Let's just say he paid for it.'

I stopped walking. 'What do you mean?'

Susan pretended to be flustered, but I could tell she wasn't really. She leaned in close. 'He had a vocation,' she told me as if we were spies in a movie, 'but … he ended up not listening to his heart and marrying a woman, and, well … unhappiness isn't the word for what he got in the end.'

'Unhappiness?' I wanted more information.

Susan looked left and right. 'Just think of the worst

consequences and it's ten times worse than that.'

My mind boggled. What would those be?

Susan softened back into the usual Opus Dei chat, quoting Escrivá and talking about herself and her own vocation. 'I just knew,' she said, 'I didn't want to be like everyone else, miserable and wasting my life. I wanted something else, something amazing.'

That sounded just like me. I wanted something amazing. But the lives of assistant numeraries didn't really seem amazing at all. There must be something about all of this that was kept secret until you joined.

'We will be visiting the Father tomorrow,' she said then, 'in his crypt.'

I didn't know what a crypt was.

'Let's say a prayer before Mass,' Susan suggested, starting the Hail Mary as we walked back. I joined in on the second half of the prayer as she repeated it over and over.

By that stage we were back at the place we were staying and everyone was getting ready for Mass.

In Mass I tried to channel this young woman with a 'strong vocation' who these women seemed to see. I closed my eyes and concentrated on the sermon, translated after every line into other languages. But I still didn't understand any of it at all.

Josemaría Escrivá was buried in Rome, in a marble crypt under the altar in a church called Our Lady of Peace. Miss O'Rourke had shown us photos of his dead body lying in state in the *Noticias* and I was afraid he would still be there, on view. Thankfully he wasn't.

The church that held his crypt was cold and dark. There were large murals on every wall. This was totally different to our church in Ballyvourney, which had plain plastered walls, and the little oratory in Ballyglunin with its plain decor. This church was ornate and opulent. There were columns and mosaics, marble and gold everywhere. But even with all of those riches, it was cold and unfeeling inside. It echoed and felt unfriendly and dour. I longed for Ballyglunin and our lovely oratory with its big window, where everyone shoved in on the small pews and said the Mass together. In here people said nothing. I had nothing to say either, because I felt nothing inside of there.

Behind the altar I set my eyes on a beautiful painting of Our Lady and little Baby Jesus: at least that was something. She looked so happy with her baby, and I felt something there. The love that I would give a baby bubbled up in me as I looked at Jesus' little hands and feet. I really wanted to be just like Mary, a devoted wife and mother. Being some solitary worker in the background of this organisation seemed like the exact opposite of how I saw my life. I hated the work in Ballyglunin. Surely a life like that of Mary, the Mother of God, could be a vocation – surely that was my vocation. How could I be getting this so wrong?

Fourteen

The sexes don't mix in Opus Dei, but in Rome at the Pope's gathering for UNIV (an annual gathering for students organised by Opus Dei), we would see from afar the boys our age who were coming and going just like we were. We passed them constantly, our groups and theirs. They looked so clean and well put together. Everyone at UNIV smelled of Nenuco, a Spanish cologne that smelled like lemon and fresh air. Back then I loved the smell of it. Miss O'Rourke and Miss Smith always smelled like it too, spraying it on their clean clothes from little squeeze bottles.

I tried my hardest to look good too, keeping a hairbrush in my bag and attempting to put together proper outfits from what I had. Secretly I wanted one of these young men to see me and for us to fall into a clandestine romance. I imagined meeting him down in the crypt and making plans to marry with him behind the tomb. My heart raced at the thought of that.

Maybe it would come true if I was in Opus Dei. Maybe I could be like the women I had met down at Ballyglunin who filed past us as we cleaned the hall, wedding rings on their fingers, smiling and happy, waving out the door to their husbands who had dropped them off for the get-togethers, recollections and retreats. I supposed I could be a supernumerary, and have it all.

'Opus Dei can be your family,' Miss O'Rourke said when I told her what I was thinking.

'No, I mean I want a husband,' I said, 'and a … uh … family …'

She looked appalled. I ran over the words in my head to check I hadn't accidentally said something explicit.

'Impure thoughts are a mortal sin and belong in the confessional,' she said, and looked away in disgust. I was mortified, right down to my toes. I hadn't been thinking anything, except for the real hope that I – like most girls want to – would get to have a wedding. I never raised that desire again with any of them just in case. And I tried to pray to God in my head, to explain myself, but I couldn't figure out how. Was I supposed to talk while I prayed? Nobody else did. Was it imagining a conversation in the hollows of my mind? Wasn't that just pretending? It was all so hard.

'A vocation as big as a house,' Miss Smith told me over and over again. She said it to everyone as soon as she introduced me. I tried squinting to show I would have to think about it. I couldn't find the feeling she was so sure I had inside of me. I didn't know what a vocation was, because it clearly wasn't what I dreamed about.

'A vocation feels like you really want to be a good person,' Susan said when I asked her, 'and it is when you know you love God – don't you?'

I supposed I did. I said I did.

Susan pressed the point. 'So if you do love God, how can

you refuse His gift for you? His gift is your vocation. Don't deny yourself God's love. Write and ask for permission to join Opus Dei, then you will know.'

The truth was that I didn't know what on earth she was talking about. I wondered all the time what God was. Everyone talked as if they were sure of what it was. But I never felt like I knew, even when I was in these ornate churches in Rome. I felt something, awe maybe, but was that God? The light coming through stained glass? I'd felt the same feeling when I saw Liberty Hall in Dublin, and God had nothing to do with that one. Maybe it was all God, maybe none of it was. I didn't know at all.

I kept thinking about how much Miss Smith and Miss O'Rourke wanted me to write this letter, and now Susan. They seemed so excited about it and when I hummed and hawed they flocked around me, encouraging me to do it. The attention was nice.

'I don't know what kind of numerary to be,' I said that first evening in Rome, on the way to supper. I was being left out of the conversation.

'You'll ask to be an assistant numerary,' Susan said, leaning across another girl to tell me. Miss Smith agreed. She made satisfied sounds when Susan said that, and then repeated the word 'definitely' over and over.

But I didn't want to be an assistant numerary, and both of them kept saying that as if it was a given. Maybe when it came to it, I decided, I could write the letter and say I wanted to be a supernumerary. This was a childish solution to a very complicated emotional problem.

And so that became my plan. I would write the letter, sure, but I would ask to be a married member. Nobody had to know. And it wasn't as if I could join now: I had to finish my course, at least.

But Susan had a pen and paper with her on our first morning in Rome. 'We should write your letter.'

I stalled and didn't take it off her. I wanted to write it by myself; I wanted to write 'supernumerary' and put it in the envelope and lick it closed.

Susan looked impatient.

'Anne Marie,' she said, and rolled her eyes, handing the pen and paper out to me again.

So I took it, and we leaned on a window ledge and I wrote it, with Susan dictating every word.

'Dear Father,' she said and paused while I wrote that down. 'Next line, I respectfully request …' she spelled the word, 'e … s … t … request admission to Opus Dei as …' I caught up, 'an assistant numerary.'

I wrote it all as neatly as I could. My heart was hammering in my ears.

'Next line,' Susan said, pointing a finger. 'I have prayed very hard … and I am sure this is my vocation … v … o … c … a … t … i … o … n … and I ask this freely …'

I swallowed over and over as I wrote the words down. The hall started to fill with people, crowding in to get a seat at the next talk. Anna, my roommate, appeared near us and hovered there.

'With love,' Susan finished off, 'and sign "your daughter Anne Marie" … and your surname.'

My name written there didn't look like my own. And as

Susan licked the envelope with the gusto of a woman who had succeeded in her task, I felt like I was falling.

I looked at Susan, but it was as if there were two of her. The walls where we sat ballooned and then things went shady. I couldn't focus. Anna came closer.

What have I done?

'I think I'm going to faint,' I said, and clung to Susan's shoulder.

She nodded and helped me balance. 'God is here,' she said.

'God is here,' said Anna too.

But I knew He was not. And if He was, I wanted Him to leave.

How could He sit up there on His big chair and make me spend my whole life cleaning and cooking?

How could God ask that of me when He let other people in Opus Dei – people worse than me – get married and have great jobs and go back and forth from Ballyglunin like they were celebrities?

Why not me?

'Wait,' I said.

Susan passed the letter to Anna and it was gone, with her, into the crowd.

I felt like I could not catch my breath.

I was *in* Opus Dei.

———

We went to visit Tiburtino, the centre for Opus Dei, to look at the kitchens there. 'It is state of the art,' we were told. It was between lunch and dinner time and it was quiet. We only stayed a while.

It was arranged that we would go to this large Opus Dei centre, just outside of Rome, where the Father of Opus Dei, Don Álvaro del Portillo, was holding a get-together for female Opus Dei members and for visiting non-members. We were to get coaches there.

'You'll ask a question,' Miss O'Rourke told me at breakfast beforehand, handing me a piece of paper with a question typed out on it. I read over it. 'You ask that when the microphone is passed to you, okay?' she said. 'This is a real privilege.'

I was chuffed. I fixed my skirt and my hair behind my ears, wishing there was a mirror nearby to check my face. I pulled my sleeves down over my arms: there was a little rash on my elbow creases.

'It's probably from the heat,' Catherine Doyle said.

We had bumped into each other and were going around together. She had started keeping seats for me at the talks.

'We should always sit together,' she said, and I was delighted.

She had been thrilled to hear I had joined Opus Dei. I still couldn't believe it, but I was encouraged by this girl acting like she and I were something to one another now. 'We're sisters now,' she had said, and did a little slide with her foot to my side.

Everything Catherine said and did felt cool to me. I tried to copy her nonchalant movements in the breakfast room.

Catherine pushed her chair back and went to get us two cups of tea, bringing them back with a big smile on her face. 'It's like tar, unfortunately,' she said putting the cups down. 'A

Dubliner must have made it' – we both giggled at her cheek – 'but at least we can add loads of milk.'

She poured it and I pulled the little sugar bowl across by the handle and opened it. It was empty.

'Oh!' I said, and reached across behind me to the next table and lifted the lid of theirs. It was full of sugar, so I took it to our table and stirred two spoons of it into each of our teas. Then I noticed Catherine staring at my hand, so I stopped stirring.

'Anne Marie,' she said, 'don't be lazy. Go and get the right thing at the right time.'

'What do you mean?' I asked.

Catherine just shook her head, stood, lifted the sugar bowl and replaced it on the table I'd taken it from. She took our sugar bowl and went up to the main buffet and filled it from the larger bowl of sugar that sat there.

As she returned with it, my face felt so hot. I'd done the wrong thing. I pinched the skin on my knees and tried to look like I didn't care. But I could feel myself blush.

'Gosh, girl,' Catherine said, 'have you never had a fraternal correction before?'

I shook my head.

'In Opus Dei we say, "Wounds from a brother are better than kisses from a stranger,"' she told me, 'and so we help one another to perfection, we speak to each other as God would, and it makes us all more perfect in His likeness.'

I didn't see why taking the sugar was something God would give a shit about.

'It's the little things, Anne Marie,' Catherine said, as she sat down. 'These little things matter, you know?'

I did know. Miss O'Rourke was always saying that same thing. But never to me. In Ballyglunin the 'little things' comment was only ever rolled out for the other numeraries. In Ballyglunin, I felt like a golden girl. But here, the golden girl was Catherine.

Catherine explained that within Opus Dei, 'fraternal correction' is a practice where one member charitably advises another to help them improve in their spiritual life or moral conduct.

'Matthew 18:15,' she said.

I felt a push from within to make myself look and act as perfectly as Catherine did.

So as we headed to the lectures, I was extra careful.

In the conference centre there were long marble corridors that stretched into a large auditorium with a stage. It was bustling, like Connolly Station on a Friday evening, with hundreds and hundreds of women from all over the world. I saw Japanese girls in traditional dress. There were all sorts of Europeans, and many Canadians and Australians – and us. You could spot the actual members of Opus Dei, all dressed well and smiling widely, and seeming to know what would happen next. You could also spot the recruits, all wide-eyed and accompanied by members.

We filled the room, some of us on chairs and some of us on the floor. Miss O'Rourke sat on a chair, behind myself and Catherine on the floor. I looked around.

And when the 'Father' and his huge entourage entered the conference hall, the female Opus Dei members got delirious, like he was some rock star and they were teen girls. They stood up, clapping with happiness, stifling their squeals with their hands as he stood at the top, looking down at us all. Then he started to speak. Dotted around the room were translators who repeated his lines in other languages, including English. My interest in this man soon diminished. His lecture was impossible to follow and bored me to tears.

My head hurt from Miss O'Rourke translating from Spanish to English into my ear, and my neck hurt from bending over to hear what she was saying. At one point I leaned back and she asked if I could hear. I told her I could and totally zoned out instead. I picked a hole in the carpet.

When del Portillo eventually stopped talking, applause erupted. I looked around in surprise. Everyone in this place was on some other level to me – they had to be. I hadn't understood anything of any of it.

The questions started then. Miss O'Rourke was giving me a look, and I didn't understand what she wanted, but I soon realised that the piece of paper was to be handed back. I watched her give the microphone and question to another girl. My heart raced as I looked for a smile from her anyway, and I relaxed when I got one. Me and her were sisters now too, right?

I sent postcards home. I just wrote that Rome was lovely and that I had eaten spaghetti and Italian ice cream.

Fifteen

I told Niamh what I had done as soon as I saw her. She seemed to think it was a good thing. She congratulated me and seemed happy about it, at least.

'Wow, Anne Marie,' she said, 'that's great. You are one of them now.'

'Don't tell your parents,' I said. 'They'll only tell my parents.'

'You're not going to tell them?' Niamh asked.

'Not yet,' I said. 'I will in person, when I am ready.'

'So,' she said then, 'we aren't going to London, I suppose?'

'Oh,' I said, 'we will! Let's still go!'

'How can you if you're a member of Opus Dei now?'

I hadn't really thought about that.

'I don't think things will change much,' I told her. 'Sure doesn't Miss O'Reilly have a job?'

In that moment I thought maybe that was true. Maybe I could get my diploma and go to London or work in the Grand again. Nothing had to change, right?

I was so wrong. My whole life had done a flip-reverse, and I was not going to have my own life for a long time.

You see, in Opus Dei there is something they call 'The Norms'. The Norms are the rules for how you live day-to-day as a member of the organisation.

In the morning, when you woke up, you had to observe what Opus Dei called the 'heroic minute', getting up immediately when you were called, kissing the floor and saying the word *'Serviam'*. I was never totally sure why. Then you made your bed, and then you showered. 'Glorified be suffering,' Miss Smith said when she instructed me on how to shower every morning. Part of the Norms was that you had to wash daily, in a three-minute shower, with at least a minute of that to be in freezing cold water. Once a week I had to sleep on the floor.

'Do I get a board for my bed?' I asked and was told no. Only female numeraries got the board. Male members of Opus Dei and assistant numeraries sleep on the floor.

'Once a week,' I was told, 'and on another night you should forgo your pillow.'

Then twice a day you were expected to pray in silence in front of the tabernacle in the oratory. You did that for 30 minutes, and then at some stage in the day you were to do a timed spiritual reading for 15 minutes. You'd read something by Escrivá, usually. But what he wrote is limited and so we would read the same things over and over. Then, at some stage, usually during my work, I had to say the entire rosary. That's the Apostle's Creed, six Our Fathers, six Glory Be's, and 53 Hail Marys.

Oh, and *one* Hail Holy Queen.

I was expected to do 14 decades of the rosary while I was cleaning and cooking, and then in the evening I would join the others to say the last decade. I had to go to Mass daily, of course, and we recited the Angelus twice a day in Latin, at noon and 6.00 p.m., stopping our work and looking at an image of Our Lady. We had to go to an Opus Dei priest for Confession every week, meet with our spiritual directress for our weekly chats, and speak to the priest once a week outside of the confessional too.

I had to observe total silence from two o'clock until six o'clock every day, and then from ten at night until the following morning at eight.

In the evening I was expected to read more by Escrivá and go to visit the tabernacle again to think and pray.

Then we had Benedictions on a Saturday. I still don't know the purpose, not exactly, but there would be a list of people to pray for, and the Host, that large Communion, would be on view.

My mother was always on the list, even though I never put her there.

There was no time to think in the organisation. There was no time to be Anne Marie, I was just another drone, repeating words I didn't understand like a never-ending buzz from morning to night, working for someone I couldn't see or know. For nothing.

I plodded through every week, each day a replica of the one before. I was jaded from the dullness and I could never really get the hang of this praying, I'll be honest. My imagination would run almost as soon as I'd shut my eyes and I'd daydream most of the time. Then I'd feel really guilty about it.

On top of all of that routine and prayer, every single day – twice a day – we would meet with other numeraries in the get-togethers. We had one at three and another at nine-thirty.

I found it really hard, especially observing the silent parts of the day, staying out of the joking and gossip as I worked with the girls.

Oh, and once a week I had to attend a very long talk called a 'circle' on some topic like mortification, charity, promiscuity or the like, and sometimes (most times for me) you'd be told to confess a sin, the details of which were decided by your spiritual director – in front of everyone.

It was the first thing that I went through when I came back from Rome.

'Anne Marie,' Miss Smith called to me after Mass, 'did I see you giggling during prayers there?'

She had. The priest had been saying the prayer seriously and his voice cracked and broke, making a yodel sound over the word 'Alleluia'. It was my first morning back and I had been elated to see my friends and the familiar house I loved.

When the priest's voice croaked, I caught Niamh's eye and the two of us, always with the same sense of humour, though desperately trying to restrain ourselves, descended into giggles. Sharon was sitting shoulder to shoulder with me and I could feel her shaking and knew she had caught the bug as well.

I was in for it as soon as I caught Miss Smith's evil eye across the room.

'And you didn't wear a mantilla,' she said, when she corrected me in the get-together in front of Miss O'Rourke, Miss Byrne and Miss Diaz.

'I didn't remember to,' I said. It was my first day, after all. I gave her a little smile, hoping to see the usual warmth. There was none.

'You must show leadership, Anne Marie,' she said, 'now that you are a member of Opus Dei.'

These corrections didn't feel like a nudge in the right direction; they felt like ritual humiliations.

So after that first day, I stopped sitting with my classmates in Mass at all, and sat with the members of Opus Dei. I was one of them now, wasn't I? I sat with the directors in the oratory, and inside of my head I talked to God, but it was babble, bits of prayers and sentences that didn't even make sense.

I was pretending.

After Mass in the morning, I would go back and become a classmate again. But it wasn't the same. There was something that smelled suspicious about me now; I could see that was the case. The girls talked among themselves and stopped when I came close. Only Niamh would give me a wink or a wave. But I saw her as someone who could get me into trouble, so I stopped waving back.

On the green bus in the mornings I would sit beside Miss Smith and we would say the rosary all the way to Gort Ard.

'I wondered about my things,' I said to Miss Smith, after a few days in Ballyglunin under my new regime of devotion. I had noticed my little things from home were gone. Nothing worth anything – a couple of photos, one of me and the showband star Johnny McEvoy that I had taken in the hotel one night when he was performing in Killarney at the Gleneagle Hotel.

'Things?'

'The things in my room,' I said, 'my photos and little things. Did someone take them?'

But I knew the directors had.

'Those things,' Miss Smith said, 'are links to your previous life, far from God. You would only be distracted by those things.'

'I wouldn't be, I promise,' I said and I meant it. 'If I can have my things I promise not to even look at them.'

'If you're not going to look at them,' Miss Smith countered, not taking her eyes off the road, 'why do you need them?'

I couldn't think of an answer.

'What about my book?' I asked her then. 'I hadn't finished it.'

'All the books you will ever need are in the sitting room.'

I knew the books that were there were all just various publications by or about the same person – Josemaría Escrivá.

Miss Smith started another prayer then.

That was that.

When we got to Gort Ard to start work Miss Smith pulled me aside. 'Now,' she said, fussing with her bag as she spoke, trying to shove the keys into the side pocket. She gave up and shoved them into her coat. 'Anne Marie, remember to do your Norms, all right?'

I nodded.

'Don't mind the others,' she told me, with a pointed finger toward the door where my classmates were going through to the house – each of them looking at me with eyes that asked me who I was now. I could tell Niamh had filled them in.

They looked at me as if they wanted to know where their friend was gone.

But the truth was I didn't know.

———

'If I wanted to be a different sort of member,' I asked one evening at a get-together, 'can I?'

Miss O'Rourke and Miss Smith looked at each other when I asked that, and Miss Diaz just acted like I hadn't spoken. None of them answered me then. They never answered that question, but on the way to work the next day Miss Smith told me once again that she had never seen a vocation like mine. It's hard to argue with someone who insists. I never found a way to cut through, never knew how to say to them they had it all wrong.

'It's as big as a house,' she said again, and as I got out of the car she said, 'Now don't forget to do your Norms.' She said that every morning from then on.

She had gone from being called my tutor to being my spiritual director. I felt forced to confess things I would usually keep to myself, like bad feelings I might have, or thinking about boys, which Opus Dei called 'impure thoughts'.

These conversations usually took place in the directors' bedrooms, and now that I was a member of Opus Dei they were referred to as *charla*, the Spanish for 'chat'.

I hated them, those *charla*. They gave me this awful feeling, an agitation that sent my fingers to find anything on my skin or nails to pick at. I was always trying to give these women the 'right' answer. But I didn't know what that was, not until I saw the smile. So I was constantly playing a game of blush, not knowing what they wanted from me, but always trying to pinpoint it, always trying to tell them what they wanted to hear.

And there was something else, something darker. Something I still cannot get my head around all these years later at all.

―――――

'Anne Marie,' Miss O'Rourke called to me from her bedroom one evening, 'I need to give you something for your Norms.'

She closed over the door behind me as soon as I came in (but left it ajar). On her desk was a small linen bag with a drawstring and a small tag. She lifted it and pulled it open and pulled out a small twisted rope, like a thick plait that had come loose on one end.

'This is for your mortifications,' she told me, and placed it into my hand.

I stared at her. I knew what the word meant; she had told me before it was the reason she had no mattress. It was the reason I had cold showers too. Miss Smith had explained about how suffering was glorious.

But I didn't know what this thing she was giving to me was. It looked like a whip for a horse.

'What is it?' I asked.

'This is called a "discipline",' Miss O'Rourke said, and put her hand back into the bag, pulling out a metal chain with a clasp holding it together, 'and this is the cilice.' There were spikes on the metal links, and she held it up.

It looked like something you would put on an animal. I'd seen something like that on the neck of a dog.

'You wear this,' she said, 'on your leg for two hours every day.'

I balked. What on earth did she mean?

She flattened the spikes against her leg. 'It goes on this way, spikes in,' she said. When she looked up and saw the horror on my face she softened and told me, 'All of us here in Opus Dei do these mortifications.'

She stood up straight and put a hand on my shoulder. 'It helps us to resist the want for comfort and to avoid temptation,' she said. 'In Opus Dei we want to volunteer to be uncomfortable, to be closer to Christ.' She handed me the bag with the chain back inside. 'Pop the cilice on every single day after lunch, and take it off before dinner. No longer than that, all right?'

I was still holding the twisted rope – the discipline. I held it up.

'What is this for?' I asked her, but I knew what it was for.

She took it and lifted her arm over her head, with her other hand on the back of her skirt. And this look took over her face, where her eyes rolled back in her head, like the face of saints in paintings as they're burned alive. She held the cord up and then snapped her arm back and she lashed herself on the backside, over her skirt, three times. Her eyes eventually closed and her mouth moved a little, a prayer.

I shuddered.

'We mortify ourselves, Anne Marie, onto our bare flesh,' she said, handing it back to me, 'and we do it daily. The cilice is to be done every day, the discipline once a week. On bare flesh, all right? And we do *not* discuss our practices with outsiders, all right?'

Then she dropped the whip into the bag and drew the strings together and tied it. She handed it back to me.

146

'Now, some housekeeping,' she said, 'pardon the pun.' I smiled, but she didn't. 'As an assistant numerary you need to learn the ropes from the others, from the best we have. There is an Opus Dei centre you will go to. I'm not sure when that will be organised, but you'll be going up there at some stage.'

I nodded an okay. I was holding the bag she had given me away from my body, my hand tight around the top of it like it was the ears of a dead hare.

'Okay,' she said, and opened the door. I went through it and she said after me, 'Cilice every day, Anne Marie.'

I walked fast to my room and shoved the bag under my pillow as fast as I could, feeling the spikes of the cilice through the cloth. I stared at the cross on the bedroom wall.

Niamh and Sharon came around the door, and I shoved the bag further in, down the side of the bed.

Sixteen

'God, I'm so bored,' Sharon said, and she fell back onto her bed with such force that her legs came up and she showed her knickers. When she realised, she sat up and burst out laughing; we all did. Once girls' laughter gets into the air it becomes contagious, and before we knew it we were all humming the air of a pop song by Blondie and dancing with each other around the bedroom.

'Da da da,' Niamh sang as she grabbed my hand and we twirled under each other's arms.

Mary Donovan ran to the other room and came back fast with a camera, breathless, saying she had forgotten to take any pictures this whole year and that she wouldn't want to forget our faces when we left, 'so … cheese!'

She held it to her eye and we all turned and posed together, arms slung over one another, big smiles and happy faces. The camera whirred and a photograph appeared out of the front of it, which we grabbed and squealed over as the light developed it, revealing Sharon at the back making a funny face. I remember that I looked so happy in it, smiling with my arm around Niamh.

I'd love to have that photograph, that last smile of my childhood.

'Go again!' Niamh said, grabbing the camera and pushing Mary into the group.

Sharon threw herself back onto the bed, the same move that started this all off, and I followed her. So did Mary.

'Cheese!' Niamh shouted, laughing, and we knew she wasn't serious, so we kicked our legs and Mary slid onto the floor as if she had died suddenly, and I could feel my breath going with the amount of laughing I was doing. I rolled over onto my tummy, and then the door burst open and suddenly Miss Boyle – of all people – was in the room.

'Girls!' she shouted. 'Put that camera away now!'

We all sat up, pulling our nightdresses and dressing gowns down as fast as we could, shoving our feet into our slippers, which had fallen off.

Miss Boyle had her eyes squeezed shut and both hands pressed against her chest.

She backed out of the room and a minute later Miss O'Rourke arrived.

'Anne Marie – my bedroom now, please?' she said, without opening her eyes. She turned around and walked away down the landing, leaving the door of our room open.

I looked around at the girls, half wanting to laugh, half wanting to blame them somehow. The whole way down the hall my mind raced to find a way to blame them. But nothing came to me. It had been fun, it had been harmless.

'Close over the door,' Miss O'Rourke said. She stayed standing. I kept myself in the doorframe.

'What has Miss Boyle told me?' she asked, and her hand went to her chest. 'A member of Opus Dei ... committing a mortal sin ... I ...'

I wrinkled my nose up. 'I was not!' My hands balled into fists at my sides.

'It was so,' she said again. 'A member of Opus Dei committing mortal sins in this house … I … well, I …'

I don't think I had ever seen Miss O'Rourke so upset – but she had it all wrong.

'We were just messing,' I said. 'We weren't doing anything at all, I promise.'

'Have you lost your mind?' Miss O'Rourke asked. 'The immoral photo Miss Boyle saw … being taken …'

'I was on the bed,' I said, feeling my breath speed up and fill my lungs so full I felt like they would burst. It wasn't immoral. It was just messing. My vision distorted, blurred, as my eyes filled with tears. There were two of everything.

'It is an absolute disgrace,' she said, 'you, an assistant numerary, committing mortal sins … Where is that photograph?' she asked, holding out her hand as if I had it with me.

'Niamh has it,' I said.

She pointed. 'Go and get it right now, right now.'

I hurried back to the room. Niamh and Sharon were lying down with their blankets tucked under their chins. They sat up when I came in.

'They want it – where is it?' I held one hand out and patted it with the other.

Niamh pointed at the dressing table, where I saw the photo leaning against the glass.

'Is that it?' I asked. 'Didn't we take two?'

She nodded. 'Mary has it.'

I left and went to Mary's room, retrieving the photo out

straight of her hand and bringing both to Miss O'Rourke in her room.

She didn't even look at them; she just scrunched them in her hand and fired them into the bin. 'You are in a serious state of mortal sin,' she said, gritting her teeth and twisting her face as she said it.

I filled with fear and she noticed.

'If I were you I would do some serious talking with God before you close your eyes, Anne Marie,' she said. 'That is what I would do.' She blessed herself. 'Now go to bed. I will see you in the morning outside the oratory.'

I ran back to my room. Sharon had the lights out already. I pulled off my slippers and knelt on the ground to say my prayers.

Miss O'Rourke's voice replayed in my head: 'You are in a serious state of mortal sin.'

'Anne Marie?' It was Niamh. 'Are you okay?'

It made me angry that she was asking. I turned on my knees.

'Stop snooping!' I shouted at her, anger flooding my head. She had been the one to ask for the second photo, she was the one coaxing the Devil, not me. 'Just go away and mind your own business.'

I saw the shape of her sit up in the bed. 'Are you crying?'

I held my lungs still, breathing through my nose.

'Go away,' I said again.

She stared at me through the dark. 'Your dad keeps asking my mam when you're coming back, when he sees her like.' She scratched her nose. 'Should I just tell him ... you've joined?'

'Don't you dare!' I pointed at her, breaking all the rules

since it was past ten o'clock and I was supposed to be silent. 'I told you I will tell them, or I'll tell something on you!'

Neither of us knew what that would be, but it was a threat that worked. She lay back down again.

I got into bed and said Hail Mary after Hail Mary after Hail Mary until eventually, a long time later, I fell asleep.

———

In the morning before Mass, Miss O'Rourke was waiting for me outside the oratory and crossly told me that the priest was waiting for me to hear my confession. 'What you did was a mortal sin,' she repeated.

My brain was mush, I was exhausted, I had done nothing, I had just been messing. And so, I followed her to the confessional. She went in first for a few minutes and when she came out I went in.

'Bless me, Father, for I have sinned,' I said, as the little door slid back and I saw the dark form of the priest lean in. He sent a shadow onto the wall beside me, drawn-out features of a nose and a bushy eyebrow.

'What sin have you committed?' the priest asked. He knew already.

'I took an immoral photo.' Even saying it made me feel upset because I had just been messing, we weren't being dirty. I told him what we had been doing. But even though deep down I really knew I hadn't sinned, the priest gave me so much penance for it, my knees were bruised from saying it all, kneeling on the hard floor.

When I went back to my room after breakfast I knew that my things had been gone through again. They took my new letters. They also took the bottle of shampoo out of my room, but they gave it back later with the sticker torn off.

'You have to mind yourself,' Miss Smith explained. 'There was a naked woman on the label, Anne Marie – did you not see it? It's immoral and you should have handed that in.'

I had seen it: it was a normal label for shampoo, nothing more than the shadow of a woman's shape. Most of the shampoos had something like that on them. This fear of temptation, and sinfulness, even then, disturbed me so much.

Before she went Miss Smith crossed the room and opened my wardrobe.

'This won't do,' she said, moving the items around. 'Remember what we talked about before: the state of your wardrobe is a reflection of your spiritual life.'

I felt this stir of frustration knotting in my guts. It wound around my body, and clutched at me and turned into a low-level pain. In my sleep that night I dreamed I was being squeezed by a snake.

Seventeen

'I'm thinking of whistling myself,' Mary Flanagan said one day in the green bus.

Miss Smith turned her head to give her a wide smile.

I had noticed a coldness from Miss Smith right after the photo incident. It was at first on and off, like this strange non-act that I could not be sure of. Then suddenly it was an absolute withdrawal of the warmth I had grown used to, but nothing you could complain about, nothing you could really put into words. The gushing stopped, the love stopped. Now my existence was a set of orders given coldly, always expected to do more than I could.

'You know, Mary,' Miss Smith said, over her shoulder, 'you've always struck me as someone with a very deep mind – you'd make a huge impact on the Work.'

'Really?' Mary looked pleased with that.

And a few minutes later, as she parked, Miss Smith turned fully around to Mary. 'We should go for a walk together later.'

When she said that, I just looked out the window. I loved my walks with Miss Smith outside. In Ballyglunin nobody was allowed walk around by themselves, and so I loved to go with Miss Smith. Most times we had silent walks, where I could imagine myself as a lady of the house and her as my visitor.

I still played those imaginary games in my head all the time.

Sometimes I'd pretend I was waiting for my husband. Sometimes I'd pretend the footsteps beside me were his and that we owned this house and we would go through all sorts of turmoil together. I escaped into that world as a way to cope.

'Are you still struggling with your impure thoughts?' Miss Smith cut through my dream in a lowered voice. Herself and Mary Flanagan had already done a loop around the grounds and she was doing another loop now with me. We had walked mostly in silence.

I didn't answer Miss Smith. I didn't know how to. What was I supposed to say? Yes? That I thought about boys constantly? *Yes, Miss Smith,* I imagined saying, *I'm 17.* I wanted to be hugged and danced with and twirled around.

We had been watching a movie a few nights before. I'm not sure what it was, but it had clearly passed the Opus Dei bar for what was considered 'appropriate', and Robert Redford was in it. When Redford had come on screen, Sharon had let a small squeal out of her, and then, when I saw the other girls smile in response to that, I did too.

Then I said, 'Oh my God, isn't he a fine bit of stuff altogether?' and I said it loudly.

'Anne Marie!' Miss O'Reilly stood up from her chair. 'Please come here.' She left the room and I followed her, embarrassed.

She turned on her heel. 'Anne Marie, you are a celibate member of Opus Dei and to speak about men like that is a mortal sin!'

My mouth dropped open. I wasn't even allowed say that in a room of just girls? This was rubbish. How could I get in trouble for that?

My 'lust' and 'immorality' would be their focus for a few weeks then. Catching me for a chat or a *charla* and bringing it up again and again until my head was spinning.

Now here she was going again.

'And,' she said, 'have you been doing your corporal mortifications?'

I didn't answer. I was doing them, but not with much enthusiasm. The whip hurt if you weren't careful, and it would sting so much when you put your clothes back on. I had tried to wear the cilice loose enough that it didn't damage my skin, but then it would fall off. And you couldn't wear tights with it, because the jagged metal would catch and rip them. Everyone in Opus Dei wore pop socks.

'Anne Marie,' she warned me, 'you are to do the mortifications, you must do them.'

I nodded.

'Every day for two hours the cilice,' she ran me through the routine again, 'one night per week at least on the floor, and on the Saturday night, you are to lash yourself with the whip.'

I agreed to do it. I wanted to do it; I knew it was what I should be doing to make sure I didn't let the Devil inside of me.

'And if you are thinking about boys,' Miss Smith said to finish up, 'if you're thinking about' – she lowered her head and her voice as she said this – 'impure thoughts, or … other things … holding hands, even, you must go and confess, all right? You must.'

I nodded along, promised I wasn't, but that if I did I would.

'If these thoughts come into your head,' Miss Smith said as we rounded back to the house, 'you must think very hard

156

about something else, Jesus on the cross, or the sacrifices our Father made for the Work.'

I didn't tell her about my actual thoughts, the ones I tried not to say out loud.

They did slip out sometimes, however.

'Can assistant numeraries get married?' I had asked one night, out loud in front of everyone at a get-together. I wasn't getting answers during my spiritual meetings with Miss Smith or Miss Diaz, who sometimes took me. They would ignore questions like that, skirt around them, make me feel awkward and crazy.

I was ignored again then.

But Miss O'Rourke talked after that question about the vocation of our Father's little daughters. She told us a story of how Escrivá realised that what his mother and sisters brought to his life, at home, was exactly what Opus Dei needed. They even looked after the Administrations in the first male Opus Dei centres. So he decided to ask the women in his family to bring their type of domestic service to the Work. Then he set out to recruit other women to do the same.

'By an assistant numerary following her vocation,' Miss O'Rourke said, 'and looking after her family of Opus Dei and the Opus Dei centres, she can get closer to God and to Heaven.'

'She? So it's just women?' Mary Flanagan asked. 'Why not men?'

Miss O'Rourke nodded and laughed as if that was obvious.

'The Administration is the backbone,' she said.

I thought about that word, *administration*. That wasn't what I was doing, not at all. I was serving and slaving.

————

'Thinking about marriage, Anne Marie,' Miss Smith told me at our next meeting, 'will lead you to temptation. You know what happens to people who involve themselves with the Devil … It's not good things. Think about the little boy.'

She said *boy* in a hissed whisper, and an image of a little crucified boy came into my head and I couldn't shake it. As I lay in bed that night I couldn't stop being haunted by it, no matter how I twisted and turned. My head filled with visions of the Devil, this cackling humpbacked creature with gnarled fingers coming after me, clutching at my soul and dragging it out of me into the fires behind him. I was so frightened.

It must have been a Saturday as I got up and went into the bathroom and lashed myself on the backside over and over as if I was lashing at him. I was so exhausted with pain afterwards it was easier to fall back to sleep. But when I did, the nightmares I had were way worse than my waking imagination.

'What's wrong with you?' Niamh asked me the next day in Mass.

I sat down beside her and let out a gasp as the cilice on my leg caught into the small bit of fat I had and pinched me.

'Nothing,' I said to her.

She put her hand onto my leg. 'What is that?' she asked me in a whisper.

I pointed toward the tabernacle and shook my head. I didn't want to answer. 'Mass is about to start,' I told her.

'Well it hasn't yet,' she said. 'Anne Marie, tell me what is that? Are you okay?'

I nodded and pressed my lips together.

'Are we not going to go to London?'

I rolled my eyes. 'We are training here, Niamh,' I said, 'because you signed us up to. You decided not to go to London.'

'Oh yeah,' she said. 'Sharon was telling us that someone told her,' she whispered then, close to my shoulder, and I bent my head to catch it, 'the Father of Opus Dei, yer man Josemaría Escrivá, used to whip himself so badly there would be bits of skin and blood and all on the wall of his bedroom.'

I moved away from her and told her to shush.

At our gatherings in the evenings now, instead of sitting with the girls I worked with, I sat on the other side of the room, embroidering altar cloths and praying to myself. When I let my guard down, or when I didn't think, I got a fraternal correction, the dressing-down from another member that you were supposed to say 'Thank you' for. I couldn't bear those. It felt so wrong to me to be watched for my mistakes, and to be publicly told off for them.

All those accusations, the stealing, the camera, the lust, felt so shameful, and they only seemed to happen when I let my guard down with the other girls. I always ended up laughing when I was with those girls. Part of me wanted to be back on their side and out of this mad world where I was being expected to hurt myself and pray all the time, but I didn't because it was just too hard. I couldn't stop thinking of ways to get out of this. I thought about it all the time.

I couldn't let my guard down for a minute.

———

'Phone for you.' Sharon had an air about her now, like I was about to get a telling-off. That's how it felt. But when I tell you I ran to the phone, and how out of breath I was when I reached it, because I was so afraid one of the directors would get to it and talk on my behalf like they had so many times.

'Hello? Mam?' I said.

It was my dad. 'Your mam is at home asleep,' he said. 'She wanted to stay up to talk to you but the number was busy for a while so she went back.'

'Prob one of the other girls,' I said.

'It's just me so,' he said, 'maybe Tony if he walks by.'

I imagined my dad standing half in half out of the phone box across from our house.

'How are you getting on?' he asked.

'Grand,' I said.

'How's the studies?'

'Grand.' The word caught in my throat. My eyes suddenly burned with hot tears and I blinked to soothe them.

'You're over a year at it now, you must be good,' he said.

I said yeah.

'Learning what you need to make a go of it, I bet?'

'Sure am,' I said.

I held my breath. I didn't want to let him hear in my voice that I was crying. I pressed my forehead into the cool wall.

'No chance you can pop home for a weekend?' Dad asked.

I shook my head and blew the air in my lungs out slowly. 'Not yet,' I whispered. I cleared my throat. 'We have too many classes, Dad.'

'Ah sure I get it. I'd imagine you've exams coming up, do you?'

'Yeah,' I said.

I wanted to tell him I'd joined Opus Dei. I wanted to. Because I think, deep down, I knew if I told him he would come and get me and bring me back home.

I'd complained so much when I was at home, about the way my two working parents left everything to me – getting the housework sorted, doing the dinners, the laundry and tidying up. But if I could go back … It would be nothing at all. A half an hour when I got in, that's all it had ever really been. It was never like this.

But if I left … would the Devil get my mother, get my family? Would the Devil get me? Would I regret it in the end, like everyone else who ever left these people?

'I have to go, Dad,' I said.

'Ah, talk a bit longer,' he said. 'I only just put a tenpence in there.'

'I have to go,' I said again. 'I'll write to you, bye.'

And I hung up the phone.

———

'Now does anyone need anything in town?' Miss Diaz asked later at the get-together. 'I will be going in tomorrow.'

I raised a hand.

'I need to get some new shoes,' I said.

Miss Diaz stared at me.

'I'll talk to you after this, Anne Marie,' she said. 'Right now we need to discuss the apostolate.' She looked very sad about it. 'We want to get to know people,' she said, handing around bundles of little cards, inscribed with prayers and sayings. 'When we get to know someone new, we can give them these prayers, a prayer card of the Founder. Also, we will all need to have a good Saint Joseph's list.'

I remembered this list from the year before, although I hadn't partaken in it then. It was a list of three people you knew who might be convinced to whistle for Opus Dei.

We were told to use every opportunity to recruit new members. Opus Dei called it 'the apostolate'. We were often sent out onto public transport and told to look around for a girl or woman who looked friendly but alone.

'Smile at them,' the directors told us.

'Be that person,' Miss O'Rourke said. 'Get into their seat beside them, and find a way to say hello.'

She looked at me. I must have looked scared of the idea. 'If you feel shy,' she said straight to me, 'think of the Father and how he wanted us to capture souls for the Work; we must spread the word of the Work all over the world.'

'You know, choose to sit beside someone who looks young, someone who looks friendly,' Miss Diaz would tell us, 'and now, girls, remember – look for well-dressed, good-looking people, no hobos!'

'Women, girls, well dressed,' Miss O'Rourke repeated. 'You know, someone might look a bit upset, so sit down, ask, talk to them.'

Miss Smith carried on. 'People need to find the right path.' These were rehearsed lines. 'The Founder says we must always be for the apostolate – the people, we need to help them, show them, be their friend, because this is their time of need, people are lost, like lambs, and as our Father said, "May your behaviour and your conversation be such that everyone who sees or hears you can say: this girl reads the life of Jesus Christ."'

'Smiling, friendly!' we were reminded. 'Don't think you need to do it all in one go – make friends first, give them a prayer card and get their phone number!'

'Chat to people,' Miss O'Rourke said, 'make your friends, then invite them to visit us here for a meditation or a retreat.'

So I did. Myself and Mary Flanagan would go straight into recruitment mode the moment we left the centres. I did it, but I hated it. I really did. It wasn't in my nature to be outgoing. It wasn't natural to me to approach strangers. But I had Mary Flanagan to compete with and she was always getting people's names and addresses.

It was okay sometimes. For example, a woman with children was always easier, but you also knew you hadn't a shot really. On the bus she appreciated the chat and the distraction from her children. But she would be too busy then to even think about you once she got off the bus. I did what I could, and mostly just said hello to people. I was not a good recruiter, no candidate for that kind of work. I was too self-conscious, far too busy worrying about what I was doing myself to read anyone's body language. Most people ignored us or stared out the window. One or two called us Jesus freaks and told us to fuck off.

Some listened, some chatted, some lectured us back.

'You think God has favourites?' asked this old woman I had targeted in a double assault with Mary Flanagan on the bus. We had sat around her, one beside her, one in front.

'Opus Dei are God's favourites,' I said, parroting the things I had been told over and over again. 'Our Founder, Josemaría Escrivá, said that we do the Work of God. God will never leave Opus Dei members. We are his favourite children, chosen, and have a divine calling to do the Work of God.'

She raised her eyebrows, did a little jig with her shoulders. 'Well,' she said, 'that's interesting' – she leaned forward – 'because the Bible says the Jews are God's favourites. They're called the chosen ones, according to God ...' She sat back, smug, hands on her lap. 'Which is it?'

The two of us gaped at her. We didn't know. The rash on my arms was driving me mad so I just turned away and scratched it.

Later that really played on my mind, because I knew she was right. I'd read it myself in the Bible.

So I asked Miss Smith.

'I think you should pray for the answer, Anne Marie, if you don't know,' Miss Smith said, and shook her head.

'You don't even know, do you?' I burst out.

'I do know,' Miss Smith said.

'No, you fucking don't,' I said under my breath, and slammed her door after me.

Eighteen

Mary Flanagan loved her new position as the favourite. She had nothing to do with the girls at all, but she also mostly had nothing to do with me. Even when we went recruiting she barely said a word my way.

I'd been working at Gort Ard full-time with her for a while, and I knew conversations were being had about me, because Miss Smith and Miss O'Rourke knew every word I'd said of a day, and Mary always seemed to know what I was talking to Miss Smith about in the *charlas*.

I was on my own, pushed out from all sides. Niamh was the only one who even gave me the time of day now.

Mary Flanagan and Miss Boyle were always whispering to each other. This one day they were doing it at lunch. We had quiche made with the leftover veg from the night before, pressed into a round tin and baked with milk, eggs and cheese on top.

After lunch I was pairing the men's socks in the laundry.

'Anne Marie,' Mary Flanagan said, 'can I mention something to you?'

I tried to predict the correction that I knew was coming, but I had no idea.

'I noticed,' she said with a smirk and a glance over her

shoulder to where Miss Boyle was looking on, 'that you didn't pass the butter to anyone at lunch … you just ate your own dinner and at least one person had to ask you to pass it to them.'

I stared at her deadpan.

'It's very important,' she went on, 'to be sensitive to other people's needs. You really must do better, Anne Marie.'

I tried to calm the reaction that started in my chest and crept through my entire nervous system. I wanted to defend myself, to say that she had sat down herself after the whole table had butter and it wasn't up to me to think of everyone's needs when I was already eating. I hated being told off. Nothing like that ever happened to Mary Flanagan. I could never catch her out the way she did me.

But I had been told repeatedly that the saint inside me should be sensitive to other people's needs, and I was also constantly told that to be a good person I needed to take this telling-off and bring it into my heart.

So I swallowed the feelings of injustice down and tried to pray in my head, like Miss Smith had advised me to do if I ever felt that I was going to commit a sin. This boiling feeling, this hot feeling in my bones, it had to be the Devil. The way I wanted to ball my fist up and thump Mary Flanagan in her smug face, that was sinful pride. I needed to counteract it. I needed to … I wanted to be good.

I stared at the ground for the few seconds it took to say a short prayer: *Please, sweet Jesus, help me learn to be good.*

This … vocation … it suited Mary. She was so good whereas I … I just was. I hadn't goodness, but I hadn't badness either,

I didn't think. I was just going along, trying to survive, trying to be someone. I didn't know about real goodness, didn't know how to feel that way. I didn't have that sort of effort inside me either, to think about what it could be. I knew right from wrong, but it always seemed I would skip a beat and get forgetful, or distracted. And, if I am totally honest, I relied on what I knew was good or bad, as opposed to any internal measure of it.

'Thank you, Mary,' I said with gusto, beaming her a smile and picking up with the socks again.

'Well,' Miss Boyle said, coming over and giving Mary a smile as she stood beside her and put a hand on her shoulder. Then she said, 'Anne Marie is off to Dublin tomorrow to learn the ropes.'

The ropes? Tomorrow?

Miss Boyle took a sharp breath through her nose. 'Did you not know? You're going to the training centre in Dublin.'

I did not know.

'Yes,' I lied, 'Miss O'Rourke told me ages ago.'

———

'Will it just be me going?' I asked Miss Smith later in our *charla*.

She looked like it was a strange question. 'I'd imagine everyone is going if it's training.' She told me she hadn't heard about it, and as I went to leave, she asked, 'Have you done your night on the floor this week, Anne Marie?'

Opus Dei members sleep one night a week on the floor as mortification. But my attempts to sleep on the floor hadn't worked out so far: it was too cold and uncomfortable and I had crawled back up into my bed after an hour.

I said I had.

She tilted her head. 'Have you?'

I shook my head. 'Sorry, I thought you meant last week.'

'Do it tonight,' Miss Smith said, 'and make this your night for it every week, all right?'

They were always saying 'All right?' as if it was a question, but they didn't mean it. They didn't care if I was all right at all. Not even for one second.

I told Niamh and Sharon before bed that night, 'I've to sleep on the floor in the other room.'

They both rolled their eyes and said nothing.

'Lend me your pillow, will you?' I asked Niamh. 'My head bangs through my one.'

They were used to the madness by now.

'It's ten past ten,' Niamh said, passing me the pillow. 'Don't get caught chatting tonight, Anne Marie – I am so sick of seeing you being sent to the confessional.'

'Well, all of us are supposed to be up to some training place tomorrow,' I said, 'according to Miss O'Rourke, anyway.'

'All of us? For how long?' Niamh looked dismayed.

Sharon just rolled over.

I pretended to zip my mouth and left the room.

The floor was hard and cold and I was so tired, but no matter what I did I couldn't nod off. I kept thinking about my mattress. This thought crossed my mind, that sleeping on the floor might not mean directly on the boards, so I hopped up and pulled my mattress off the bed in that room. Then I lay on that and covered myself over. I fell straight asleep, only to be woken by a firm shake on my foot.

Miss Smith was looking in the door with a face of fury. 'Get that mattress up and get onto the floor, Anne Marie,' she hissed at me.

I didn't sleep a wink after that.

———

'We aren't going,' Sharon said, walking into the kitchen the next morning with dirty plates on a tray. 'We are staying here, according to Miss Diaz.'

'Who is?' I asked, looking from Sharon to the others.

'All of us but you and Mary Flanagan,' Sharon said. 'We have a domestic science teacher coming tomorrow,' she added, dumping the plates into the sink so they clattered against each other. I flinched.

What?

I was pissed off. Absolutely. I was the one who had wanted to improve my prospects and get out of my life. But now, I had nothing. I was going to Dublin to train, or so they said. Train as what? The girls here were getting a domestic science teacher? I wanted to do that. Why couldn't I do that?

Regardless of what I wanted, I was transferred to Dublin.

I wasn't really asked if I wanted to go, or even given much information, but as an assistant numerary that was just how it was. It wasn't the last time I was told, 'You're going here,' and that was that. I packed that morning on command and then, without much goodbye to the other girls, I was driven up.

I was 17 at this stage, a kid even in those days, not able to make my own choices. Opus Dei never spoke to my parents about the move, never asked for their approval, let alone consent. I was told to keep the details to myself, and I was told to lie.

'Dad would worry if I wasn't here in Ballyglunin,' I said to Miss Smith, when she told me I was going. 'He thinks I'm here.'

'There is absolutely no reason to worry him,' Miss Smith said. 'You'll be back at some stage, so for now when he calls for you we will take a message, send it up, and then you can call him back. You're one of us now – we are your family. There is no need to worry anyone. We will help you with what to say to your family when the time is right.'

Why did this feel so, so wrong?

There would be about fifteen girls living in Rathmore when I arrived. All of them were members of Opus Dei, like me, and all were assistant numeraries, like me.

'These girls are well travelled,' Miss Smith said as she was driving me up. 'They travel all over Ireland to work in the Administrations of our residences. You will, too.'

Administrations? I knew by now what that was. That was waitressing and cleaning. So I knew what I was in for. This was no training place she was driving me to: they were just going to make me a better slave.

I wasn't wrong, but it was worse than I could ever have imagined. Rathmore was a huge Victorian redbrick house, one that should have been done up inside with lush carpets and wallpaper, but instead was basic and blank and utilitarian. Inside it felt like a prison.

We arrived in the evening, just as the group of girls who lived there were shepherded in for a get-together, timed well so I could be introduced to them and they to me. I recognised Catherine Doyle, and she raised a palm to me as I came in and sat down. There were some other girls there who had whistled in Rome at UNIV. I recognised them and they recognised me, but it didn't feel good to me to be there even so. I felt trapped the minute I went inside and noticed the door locked after me.

Miss Smith spoke to the other directors in an office off the corridor and then left without a word to me.

'Our Father was halfway up the mountain—' A numerary called Mary Goretti De La Luz, the director of this centre, was telling a story. As always, the subject matter was Josemaría Escrivá and his life. I knew all of these stories; I had heard them again and again in Ballyglunin over the past two years. They were always the same and I still didn't get them or enjoy them.

In this one, Josemaría Escrivá had been climbing in the Pyrenees in Spain when he came across a wooden rose lying on the rocks.

'And as he reached out for it,' Miss De La Luz said, 'the rose came alive in his hand as a real flower. This was Our Lady's blessing.' Her face was so solemn and her eyes closed on the final few words.

As always, I didn't get that story. It came alive? Really? Was it growing? Or was it cut, and if so, with what? And how did he know it was Our Lady who blessed him? What had she to do with mountains and roses? At that time, to me, this was a sign of my own ignorance, and so I asked no questions.

Looking back, I can see I didn't believe it, but at that time the message that I took was that I was not as clever as the others. Now, I think they were pretending too.

Because nobody on earth can truly believe these cartoonish stories as real. Can they?

Miss De La Luz finished up her talk with some instructions to the girls regarding the chores they had to do before bed. She had watched me coming in with Miss Smith and seen her leave, and knew I was sitting there alone in the corner, just behind everyone. But she didn't say anything to me at all.

'Right, girls, down to prepare supper now, all right?' she said, and clapped her hands, and then she looked straight at me and left the room. I felt totally at sea.

Some of the girls looked at me. One or two said hi as they followed her out of the room. I sat there for a minute, and then I jumped up and followed too. When I got into the kitchen after the group, I was immediately handed an apron and brought into the fold by an older girl – and put straight to work.

'You can take that side,' she said, and started handing out chopping boards and then vegetables. I knew this territory.

'Where did you come down from?' she asked.

'Ballyglunin,' I said.

'Ah,' she said, 'I did a course there a few years ago – it's how I joined Opus Dei.'

'Me too,' I said, feeling perhaps a sense of camaraderie or connection in that little thing that made me focus on her as an ally. It made me feel better.

'Anne Marie,' the director called to me then. She looked at my feet disapprovingly. I knew my shoes were awful: they were years old at this stage. I'd had them for the start of Second Year and I would have been in Fourth Year now.

'It is very important,' the director said, staring at the shoes, 'to have pride in our appearance.'

There wasn't much I could do, but I apologised anyway. It wasn't like I could replace them. I had no money.

'Do you need anything, Anne Marie?' another one of the directors, Miss Gonzaga, asked me one evening. I told her as well.

But nothing was done about it.

Those shoes I had on when I had arrived in Rathmore were still on my feet when I moved to another centre, Lisdara, a year later. They were worn almost through by that stage; the leather was cracked and splitting around the sides. Even though these directors and other girls knew I had no way to replace them, I was constantly fraternally corrected about dressing properly the whole time I spent with Opus Dei.

———

From Rathmore we were bused in and out of Opus Dei centres around Dublin. I worked mostly in a beautiful house called Riversdale, though I went where I was told.

Riversdale was the women's headquarters: female numeraries ran Opus Dei in Ireland from this very fancy house. No assistant numeraries lived there. We were bused over to do the work of the Administration. We used the entrance at the back of the house to get into the kitchen, servery and laundry.

At half-six every morning our alarm call was a banging on our doors by the director. We would get ready and go to Mass, have a quick breakfast. Then onto our bus and over to Riversdale. It took about forty minutes to get there and we would say the rosary on the way.

We would bustle in and make the numeraries their breakfast, then clean up after them. We would start the housework and laundry straight after. There were women working from offices – I don't know what they did – and we never disturbed those; we cleaned for the residents and visitors and we cooked three-course lunches and dinners and prepared their breakfast then for the next day. We would eat anything they left over in the kitchen, the same way we did in Ballyglunin.

There was an Opus Dei priest who visited Riversdale every day to say Mass and to hear confessions. We looked after him too: a hot breakfast served on a silver tray, linen tablecloth, Waterford cut-glass butter dishes, the works, in one of the many beautiful sitting rooms there. When we served him we never spoke, instructed to stay silent. We would not leave for the night before checking that he was all right for everything, silently. No matter how jaded and stressed we were, we made sure that everything was perfect. It was always like that. All of the centres were like that.

Riversdale had lovely rooms, lush carpets and beautiful curtains and tiebacks, and it was warm – too warm for hard work – and we would end up sweaty and sticky by the time we got back to Rathmore. That was like a prison in comparison, cold and stark with small, hard beds and lino on the floor. The

GPO for Opus Dei slaves.

But thankfully, eventually I would always come back to Ballyglunin, even just for a while.

It was as if Ballyglunin became something of a lighthouse for me. I don't know why; maybe because of where it stood on the flat fields of Galway, maybe because it reminded me of something safe, like Niamh and home and my holidays with Auntie Bernadette. For some reason, when I could get back to Ballyglunin, I felt better. It's funny, because my life was just as miserable there as anywhere.

Maybe I felt like there, the promise I'd been made of a diploma and a course and a profession could still be possible somewhere. I would work away at these centres and dream of that house, flying myself back there in my imagination.

In those dreams it would always be just me inside of there, no other members, no girls, just me and the house waiting for something, someone. Ballyglunin and me. It felt like we were in it together.

Nineteen

In Rathmore I was shown, by example, what was expected of me.

When I first arrived there, I noticed that the dry quipping and normal messing that would go on in our kitchen down in Ballyglunin were totally absent. Nobody joked in Rathmore, nobody bitched about anyone or anything, nobody got sarcastic.

Instead, it was as if everyone acted very reverently – but like little girls. Well, not like actual little girls; I think children are quite noble in comparison to what was going on in Rathmore. In Rathmore the grown women acted like caricatures of little girls. They squealed and pretended to be frightened of things: one woman used to constantly tell me she was terrified of foreigners, and on one occasion when a delivery came with a foreign van driver she ran and hid behind the door.

Was it real?

No.

I cringe writing this, but the truth was every single one of them was putting this on. It was encouraged.

Miss O'Rourke had told me something of it, back when she was encouraging me to whistle, but I had never seen it in action. 'Our Father calls assistant numeraries his little daughters,' she had said. 'Isn't that wonderful? Little daughters.'

Things I was told never really went anywhere: I was always too busy dealing with my discomfort to take in what was really being said.

In Rathmore some women spoke in high voices and skipped from room to room and giggled in high-pitched, childish voices. They acted silly and flounced into chairs when they did the get-togethers. It made me feel sick. Of all my memories, I hate those ones the most. They'd organise to put on plays and dress up, the way children do for their parents or in school, or they'd have a fancy-dress competition judged by the directresses, who never ever took part.

Rathmore was what made me really crazy. Weeks of being dismissed by the numeraries, maybe getting a bit of attention if I acted in that childish way too, constant fraternal corrections, the restriction of my growing soul. I had never been into silliness or childishness; I knew girls who acted that way over boys, but I never did. My drive had always been to be older, to be an adult. I wanted that, the self-assuredness, so much I put it on. Laughter, from me, was always authentic.

I was whipping myself regularly and wearing the cilice every day. It was uncomfortable when I stood straight but as soon as I bent my leg at all – and working so hard meant that was constant – it was so painful it would make me limp, but when that was noticed it was like I was treated better. I slept on the floor every week, the night would be dictated by my spiritual director – whoever that was wherever I was.

I asked myself over and over, what had I done? I made the deal. Why did God have this plan for me? Maybe I could bargain my way out of this somehow. I kept thinking about Sharon and Niamh and all the other girls in Rome the year before, who had come home still having ownership over their own souls. This decision I had made pressed on my mind: it felt like I was being pushed over an edge.

Then one day, spurred on by a racing mind and a knot in my stomach, I called Miss O'Rourke on the telephone.

'I don't want to be an assistant numerary,' I told her as soon as she said hello.

'Anne Marie,' she said, 'how is it going in Dublin? Are you having a wonderful experience?'

'I don't want to be an assistant numerary,' I said again, finding it hard to inhale. 'I want to come back to my course.'

I wheezed. My throat felt like it was closing over.

'I'd say the girls love having you there,' she said.

'There's no girls here,' I said, 'just women pretending. I want to come back, Miss Cathy, I want to come back to my course.'

'Okay,' Miss O'Rourke said, 'we can talk about that next week when I come up to Dublin with Miss Smith.'

'I don't want to be an assistant numerary,' I told her again.

'You've a vocation as big as a house,' she said, and that line made me want to scream and smash the phone and bang my head so hard on the wall I would break my own skull. I gritted my teeth. She went on: 'Bigger than anyone I know. You should give yourself permission to love your vocation truly, Anne Marie.'

'What does that mean?' I spat. 'I don't want to be here.'

'Of course you do,' she said. 'Now, I will talk to you next week – we will sit down and have a good *charla*, okay? When I come up.'

She said goodbye and put down the phone. I slammed mine down, lifted it and slammed it again, and a whine came out of me, then a short blast of a roar that made one of the others pop her head out of the door nearby.

'All okay?' she asked.

I shook my head.

'I'll pray for you, Anne Marie, and for your vocation,' she told me. So rehearsed. She went back in. I really was in a madhouse.

I remember leaning my forehead against the wall and asking myself what my problem was. I wanted to understand why these women were okay and I was not okay at all. Nothing in this place made sense: the silliness, the childishness, the high-pitched voices and giggles, the hairstyles that belonged on five-year-olds. The fake adoration of the numeraries, who lapped it up. Nothing about any of it made sense to me.

I tried to think it through. Was this just me?

Then I brought into focus the others, and I thought about their lives and how they coped, or *if* they coped. I thought about working in Riversdale with the others and how sad they sometimes looked. They cried, too – I'd seen them. They lost their focus, too, and dropped things, and they got fraternal corrections, too, all the time, even from me. I was so upset, but so were they. Was this what vocation was? This struggle? Were we all feeling the same way because we were all suffering for our vocation? What was this life?

The phone rang and I ran and answered it on the first ring.

'Anne Marie?' Miss Smith's voice was kind and I burst out crying. 'Anne Marie, listen to me. I know you are struggling with your vocation. Do you know that the Devil uses our minds against us, and only when we accept our vocation as it is given to us, and offer our pain to God, can we be really happy? Offer it up, Anne Marie, offer it up.'

That was another line. Offer this up, that up, OFFER EVERYTHING UP.

Why could I not just live? Why did I have to be in a place where I couldn't breathe, where my back was bent from work and where nobody cared about me? I listened and I tried. But they didn't listen and they didn't try.

'My feet are so sore,' I cried. I still only had one pair of shoes and they were broken and ripped from constant standing and continuous work. My feet were in extreme pain, especially at the end of the day. 'I want to come back.'

'People who are truly with God, in their hearts,' Miss Smith said quickly, 'they smile at God when they suffer – sure didn't I tell you about the story our Father told about a woman with cancer, smiling to the end at God and thanking Him for sending her the pain so she could suffer more for Him?'

I remembered the story. It was about Montse, a 17-year-old girl in Spain who was a numerary and died of cancer. Miss Smith had told it to me when I had complained about the rash on my arms stinging.

'I don't want to be an assistant numerary,' I told Miss Smith now down the phone. My heart was overtaking my body, pumping blood so fast I started to shake.

'Anne Marie, you have a vocation as big as a house.' The same line over and over.

'I don't,' I said. 'Stop saying it, I don't.'

She paused, and said nothing. I heard the sound of her breathing against the receiver.

'Anne Marie,' she said very seriously, 'if you turn away from your vocation – that God has sent to you with his love – a life of misery will follow, turning away from God like this would be not only a sin ... but Anne Marie, I really promise you that you would go straight to Hell.'

That was enough for me. I was not going to bring it up again.

'Pray on it, all right?' she said in a teacherly way, and called the conversation quits, leaving me absolutely desperate in the cold hallway.

———

I was in trouble all the time.

I had let gravy boil over and since then I was being picked on till I was exhausted from it.

'Anne Marie,' Miss De La Luz came into the kitchen with a face like thunder, 'there are to be eight apple tarts served in the dining room this evening, yes?' Her accent was thick, and her eyes glared as she spat the words my way. 'If not, there will be serious consequences.'

I was on my own in the kitchen.

'Miss De La Luz,' I pleaded, 'I don't think I can do it!'

'There will be consequences,' she said, glaring at me for having the audacity to challenge her demand, and left.

Catherine ran in. 'There's visitors,' she said, 'loads of them.'

I remember praying as we made and rolled pastry, sliced

apples and got it all into the oven. We said the Hail Mary over and over as we cleaned up, one eye on the oven, the clock ticking. By some miracle we got the pies done on time and served them hot.

Miss De La Luz never so much as acknowledged how hard we worked to make that happen. When we brought the pies in, she totally ignored us.

———

I had barely seen my parents in nearly two years. One day I called them from the office with Miss Smith sitting beside me, her hand on the table ready to go for the phone should I say something untoward. She had run through the script with me just before.

'I got a special scholarship,' I told my dad, 'to go to specialised training in Dublin.'

'A scholarship for what?' he asked.

I looked at Miss Smith and she mouthed, 'Specialised training in hospitality.'

I repeated that.

'Anne Marie,' he had said, 'that's great, but we haven't seen you at all – will you get home before you go?'

Miss Smith shook her head.

'I don't think so, Dad.'

'We want you home,' he said. 'We need you here.' The way he said it, I knew things were not right at home. Something was wrong. I looked hopefully at Miss Smith.

Miss Smith shook her head really slowly.

'I have to go, Dad,' I said, letting the call go. I went back to my room and cried my eyes out.

A week later I asked to call home again. I was worried sick.

'Anne Marie,' Miss Smith said, 'what is this obsession with using the phone all the time?'

'Things are not great at home,' I explained. 'I just need to check—'

'Have you money for the call?' Miss Smith asked flatly. 'We cannot afford all of these calls.'

Of course I didn't. I had no money; whatever I got sent to me wasn't much, and it was always taken. Our families thought we earned £17 a week, and strictly speaking we did. But our board and lodgings were also £17. I never saw the money. I was just told that was the situation, and to tell my family that when they asked about money.

'I want to call home,' I said again, feeling my lip wobble.

'No,' she said.

I burst into tears. 'Let me! LET ME!' I slammed my hands onto my head and pounded them against my own skull.

'Stop that,' Miss Smith said, 'stop that!'

I pushed against her, then shoved her aside as I rushed past her. 'LET ME!!!' I screamed. I wanted to get near the phone up on the wall.

'Anne Marie!' she said, then called out for someone to come. It was Miss O'Reilly who appeared in a few moments, hearing the desperation in Miss Smith's voice.

They both stood on either side of me, not allowing me to leave the room. They stood looking at me and I could see they were praying silently, as their lips were moving. They told me

183

again that they were not letting me make a call because it was too expensive. I still cried and cried, and I was head to toe in pins and needles. My vision blurred like it had before and I couldn't see anything.

Miss Smith was cross and asked me when I was going to stop crying because there was work to be done.

The next day they allowed me call my dad at his work, but I was given strict instructions to ask one question, hear the answer and then say goodbye.

I asked Dad how everyone was and he said everyone was okay.

As I hung up the phone, I could still hear my father speaking.

Miss Smith came to the laundry immediately afterward, closed the door and told me to repeat the conversation I had with my dad. When I told her that he said everyone was fine she said, 'Look at the commotion and disruption you caused last night, and there was no need for one bit of it.'

Miss Thomas had something to say about it too. She brought me into her office and, standing looking at me, she made a face like I had been caught committing a crime. 'Miss Smith told me what your father said to you. You were hysterical, and after all of that there was nothing wrong at all.'

But I didn't believe it. I just didn't know how to get out of all of it.

Twenty

It was announced that the leader of Opus Dei, Álvaro del Portillo – the same man I saw in Rome, Josemaría Escrivá's right hand – was coming to Ireland to visit. Escrivá and del Portillo were the ones who came up with the organisation, from its Norms to all the hierarchy and the statutes and regulations. Those ideas for the public shaming ritual of fraternal corrections, those ideas for suffering being good for you, all of it. The man on his way to Dublin was one of two who decided on it all.

And again, like I had seen in Rome, there was absolute hysteria about it.

Assistant numeraries were always encouraged to be giddy and to coo and squeal when del Portillo was mentioned. Always encouraged to play at being children. Some of the older women clutched their faces and spun around when they heard his name. It was bizarre. In Rathmore you'd have thought that the Beatles were on their way, with the fanning of faces and heart-pressing that was going on with the women there. To be honest, it really confused me, because our workload had doubled.

'What's all the fuss about?' I couldn't help but ask Kate Boylan, a girl a bit older than me, who I had found swooning against the wall in the hall not long after we got the news. I had seen girls act like this before, don't get me wrong – it wasn't that. It was the person they were falling around for that I didn't get.

'It's the Father coming to see us,' she said, and rolled her eyes up to Heaven with an open mouth. The girl she was with, Pat Lynch – they were always together – did the same thing.

Then they stopped and looked at me.

'Are you not excited?' Kate asked. She stepped back from me and looked disapproving.

I didn't miss a beat, throwing my hands up and saying how excited I was too. 'I can't wait,' I said. 'Will he be coming here?'

Kate and Pat looked at each other and burst out laughing.

'Obviously not, Anne Marie,' Pat said. 'He will be going to Riversdale and we might see him there.'

'God, Anne Marie,' Kate said, 'you're so funny.'

That didn't sound like she meant it well.

There was meeting after meeting, reconnaissance-style orders delivered while overlooking the plans for movement of the leader from place to place. Del Portillo would be staying in Lismullen but would be visiting other centres, so everywhere had to be scrubbed and cleaned from top to bottom. We had to learn the times and promise that we would not be out front when he arrived, nor in the hall or on the stairs when he came in.

'Be out of the way!' we were told. 'Be unseen angels, all right?'

The meetings, well, they were actually lectures. Repetition of the rules we were to observe during the visit. Assistant numeraries were never asked for ideas or input, despite being the ones actually doing the job.

All we were asked to do was to work ourselves to death.

I'd never have thought it was possible to work harder than we already did, but it was. We were deep-cleaning every single nook and cranny of every residence in Ireland, bused in like slaves with mops and buckets. We were sent in to clean up after painters had slathered the walls; we prepped recipes and held tastings for the higher-ups to decide on his menu.

The food we planned for this guest was like nothing I had ever made before. He was to have the finest food made available to him and his favourite dishes cooked to perfection by assistant numeraries. Opus Dei knew who was on top: this was certain proof of that.

He was to eat with silver. We polished every single piece of metal in every establishment until our fingers were black.

After all of that, we also washed, dried, folded and pressed the curtains, cloths, bedclothes and towels of each house. 'Sure the man will never use all of these,' I whispered to one of the others, and got a frown. But it just seemed crazy, especially since seven days a week we never stopped cleaning anyway.

'The directors will be moving rooms,' I was told by way of explanation as to why on earth me and an assistant numerary from Carlow called Doreen Dempsey were moving furniture. 'Del Portillo should have the view and the biggest room, and' – Doreen used her knee and shoved the large bed into the right spot with a grunt – 'he should have the best bed.' She looked at it. 'I can't believe the Father is going to sleep here.' She reached out as if to touch the mattress and then snapped her hand back.

I was like Alice in Wonderland, looking around at absurdity, as grown-up women – some the same age as my own mother – pretended to faint over some … priest?! They acted like a pop star was on the way, and for sure I could have got on board with the squealing and fainting if it had been David Essex, because he was gorgeous and cool and you could daydream about him. But Álvaro del Portillo? He was an old man, balding, with thick glasses. He looked like Kojak, for God's sake. I had no idea at all what on earth the crazy-acting was about.

'Let's get this place clean as a whistle,' Miss Power, our supervisor, said on the bus over to Riversdale one morning. I wanted to roll my eyes – the place was absolutely spotless – but I pinched and picked my skin instead, staring out the window.

I had broken skin on my fingers and a bad rash around the nails. I bit the skin there to relieve the itch. There was a rash on my back as well, above my tailbone, and from breathing in the cleaning solvents and the bleach water all day my nose had developed some sort of ulcer. Earlier in the week, while cleaning a bathroom, I had splashed a tiny bit of caustic soda into my eye.

I can still see where it scarred the white of my eye.

And I wasn't the only one. On that bus I would say there wasn't one girl who didn't have a rash or some skin ailment. We never got outside sure, and we never saw the sun. We had bleeding gums and patchy, itchy skin. Sore knees. Animals in a shed, brought out to work.

I had gone to Miss Power a few times and told her that I needed something for my skin.

She had looked at my outstretched arms for a moment only

and then she said, 'I'm sure it will clear up. Offer it up!'

This morning at Riversdale she was instructing all of us over the clipboard she held in her folded arms. 'Spotless rooms, please, girls,' she called out over and over. We cleaned every inch of the place, no more or less than we did normally, but with far more vigour, and this fake excitement that felt like a charade.

I scrubbed the floors and walls with all the energy I could muster as if my life depended on it. I was starting to think maybe throwing myself into my work would solve this riddle for me. If I did what they said, if I 'gave' myself to God, maybe I would feel the things they said they felt.

And so curtains were hoovered on both sides, with assistant numeraries standing on ladders. Some of the curtains were taken down and ironed and repaired. All of the holy pictures were taken down and cleaned and dusted. Some were even replaced. The black crosses on the walls were repainted. Rugs were beaten and cleaned and swapped around, and furniture was polished until you could see your face in them. Beds and armoires were moved, rooms changed and swapped around. Sometimes the changes were decided against and swapped back on a whim, only to be redone the same way as before.

The numeraries were everywhere in their white coats, with their lists and pointing fingers, instructing all of us, the assistant numeraries, what to work on next. One in particular, Miss Power, liked to double check our work and she ruled with an iron fist.

'Remember you need to look absolutely perfect,' Miss Power told us. 'Your uniforms are your armour against the Devil.'

I knew by now that the perfect assistant numerary in the eyes of Opus Dei was as close to a robot as a human could get. We were to look the exact same every day, as best as we could, in our red uniforms and red-and-white check aprons. We were never to wear our hair in different ways, never to change our style. We were to be submissive and quiet – unless, of course, we wanted to act the baby and squeal over del Portillo. You see, if we needed to react to something with emotion, we were to channel a little girl in order to do so. We were allowed that. It was page one in the unwritten manual of how to be an assistant numerary.

I learned that by example, rewarded for the right behaviour and ignored, excluded or berated for the wrong.

I remember being given a fraternal correction for not passing the salt, then later the same day, for passing it too much. For making too much noise scrubbing, for not scrubbing properly or hard enough. For dropping the hoover, for carrying the hoover too slowly. For not closing the door quietly enough even with my arms full of linens. I was chastised, bullied, berated and lectured for not being 'perfect' but the definition would be set by each director individually, and depending on her mood. The pressure of that was immense and I could not take it.

I remember one night eating my food slowly because the day before I had been given a fraternal correction for not paying attention to others' needs at the table. Suddenly a roar was let at me, 'Anne Marie, get going NOW!' It was Miss Thomas, red faced and like a bull at the door of the dining room, demanding we jump to it to serve the female numeraries who were all sitting around their own table after coming in early. I remember how afraid I was of her as I rushed into the numeraries' dining room to serve them too late – they had been ringing the brass bell. I remember the faces they pulled as I skidded around the door – I was seriously in the bad books.

'Laziness is a mortal sin,' I was lectured for a week by my spiritual director over it, 'it is part of your vocation, Anne Marie, to care for your sisters … you have given in to sin.'

It seemed ridiculous to me but here was this whole organisation that believed in this stuff and only I who questioned it. I told myself I was lazy, and that my thoughts – that this was wrong – were the work of the Devil.

———

I was called out of the kitchen one night by Doreen.

'Your turn, Baggy Eyes,' she said, leaning in through the door. I had garnered the nickname in Rathmore because I was crying myself to sleep most nights and waking up with puffed eyelids.

I stopped what I was doing, put down the bowl I was drying and walked toward her.

'Turn for what?' I asked.

'The doctors are here,' she said, pointing down the corridor to the office. 'It's your turn.'

I put the tea towel down. 'Doctors?' I repeated.

'Doctor Ward and Doctor Faughnan,' she said. 'Do you not know them?'

I shook my head and followed her.

'Have you had your shower today?' she asked.

'Yes, of course,' I said, lifting my arm and checking my armpit for sweat. There was plenty of it. 'But that was this morning.'

She wrinkled up her nose. 'Well, just tell them you were working till just now,' she said.

I sniffed my armpit. I'd been working really hard, left on my own to iron and fold over thirty sheets. But I didn't smell bad, I didn't think.

Doreen knocked on the door of the front room, where we normally watched a film on Sundays, and opened it.

'This is Anne Marie – thanks, Doctor,' she said, and I went in.

The doctor didn't look up.

I instantly felt really alone. I wanted my mother. She always came inside of the doctor's room with me. I hadn't spoken to a doctor without anyone else there before. I didn't know what to say to this woman in her white jacket with glasses on the end of her nose. She was writing something on a small card.

'Date of birth?' she asked.

I told her.

'So ... 17?' she said, and wrote something else down. 'Right,' she said, and she turned to me, looking at my face and feeling my jawline, then behind my ears. She took her stethoscope and told me to undo the top buttons of my uniform, asking me to breathe in and out. Then she pulled a blood pressure cuff up my arm and pumped it up, all in silence, not one word to me.

'Sometimes I can't see,' I said.

'Oh?' She picked up a light and looked into my eyes. 'Well, your eyes are fine.'

I didn't say anything else on it.

'I have a lump as well,' I told her, 'under my arm.'

She checked, feeling over my shirt.

'I was working till now,' I said, to excuse the damp shirt.

'Ingrown hair,' she said as she located the lump. 'You need to wash under your arms every day.' I did wash every day, but I didn't say so, I just nodded.

'Sometimes I can't see,' I said again.

She stared at me. Then she sat down and wrote on the little card again.

'You're a good strong girl, Anne Marie,' she said, 'no reason to get out of your work.' Her tone made me feel really upset. I wasn't trying to get out of work. Was that why she thought I was saying these things? I didn't understand that.

She wrote more on her little card and then she looked up at me. 'You have quite high blood pressure,' she stated. 'Perhaps you might have thyroid issues as you get older ...' It was a commentary, not a diagnosis. I knew she wasn't going to do anything further about that. I knew what high blood pressure was. One of the Christian Brothers in my old school had it and he took pills.

'Now,' the doctor said, looking at a list, 'can you send Mary McEvoy in to me next?'

When I went outside, Mary was already waiting. I held the door for her and she went in, and then I went back up to finish the drying.

On my way back I saw a priest arrive at the front door. There was a flurry around him; the directors were whispering and blessing themselves. I lingered long enough to see one of the assistant numeraries, a girl I forget the name of, with her sleeves rolled up and scrapes all up and down her arms. Another director was bringing her in to the priest, and her eyes were red, red raw.

Twenty-one

Assistant numeraries all behave like one another and are not encouraged to do anything but their work. This is how it is for the lowest members of Opus Dei. We had to look the same, in our red uniforms, and we acted the same. We had to be submissive, always doing what we were told, never stepping out of line and always on call.

Assistant numeraries, like I was, provide a full housekeeping and administration service for the celibate and elite members of Opus Dei in Ireland. We worked from the moment we got up until the moment we went to bed, seven days a week, all year around.

And we got paid nothing.

I remember going to Rome again and lining up with this huge crowd of young women, all assistant numeraries, from all the centres in the world, and wondering what I was doing there. The Irish contingent, dressed in cheap second-hand clothing that was not suited to the warm Italian weather and made us perspire, caught the eye of someone because when we got back to Ireland we were scolded for weeks.

'They said we were grubby,' one of the other girls, Laura, said.

'Sure what can we do?' I said. 'We don't have any way to sort ourselves out.'

But after that I always did my best to look well. I always brushed my hair and rushed to get the least stained uniform.

When del Portillo, this self-proclaimed saint, finally got to us, his entourage was impressive. Priests filed in around him like some medieval Secret Service in black cassocks. Wherever del Portillo went, even to the bathroom, he was flanked by men, and we had been warned to stay back from them. To be honest, some of them were so handsome my teenage heart went into overdrive.

Del Portillo, however, was not beautiful. Our 'Father' was plain and portly and smaller than I'd thought he would be. He looked like a strict headmaster as he inspected the place where he was to be staying, looking all over it to make sure the standard suited him. I can still hear the swooshes of his and his entourage's long black skirts against their legs as they walked through luxurious room after luxurious room. I thought about Jesus and how he was born in a stable in the hay. I doubted this guy would ever even go into a stable, he looked so above anything like that.

We all felt the pressure. One slip and it felt like you'd be kicked into Hell.

Miss Duffy, the assistant numerary who mostly worked at Riversdale, and Susan, who I had met and signed up with in Rome, arrived with del Portillo. We had been briefed on these ones: as the longest-serving assistant numeraries in Ireland they had been assigned to look after all of the domestic needs for the leader during his stay. They were to be his personal assistants, his butlers, his maids.

They wore the dining-room outfits that we only ever wore for formal occasions for the time del Portillo was there – these large black babydoll dresses with aprons over them, worn with hairbands and white gloves. These were clothes that fitted them, but looked like costumes on baby dolls.

Del Portillo spent all day every day holding get-togethers for male and female members, separately, in various Opus Dei centres, including our one. We would pile in and sit down and then he would arrive in and we would stand for him, and wait to sit once he had. Everything was translated from Spanish to English, and I still do not know how anyone followed it. Were they all pretending like I was?

I never ever knew what on earth anyone was talking about. I never knew much of any of it.

———

'I don't understand the talks,' I finally admitted to my new spiritual director, Miss O'Reilly, in my weekly chat. She had a PhD in philosophy and was held in high regard as a numerary. They'd tell each other that all the time, 'She has a PhD,' as if it was a direct telephone to God. But the reality was that she never gave me answers that satisfied me. Not one of them ever did.

She always rolled out the same answer – telling me to pray on it. I told her I didn't know how to do that either.

'I look at the tabernacle,' I said when she asked me to explain, 'but it's like I can't think about anything – I need you to tell me how to actually pray.'

'If you ask God for His help,' she told me, 'He will help you.'

'Yes, Miss, thank you ...' I looked down for a moment, as if taking the information in, 'but what way do you actually ask?'

Pins and needles in my shins made me shift from foot to foot.

'To pray is to talk to God,' she said. A quote from Escrivá.

'Sure, sure.' I wiggled my toes in my shoes. 'But how do you do it ... exactly?'

'Pray on it, Anne Marie,' she said, 'just pray to God for help with this, okay?' She clapped her hands lightly together. 'Now, I will see you next week again, all right? And do not forget to do the Norms.'

I went to leave.

'Oh!' she said suddenly. 'I forgot to tell you, you're going to do a special course in the Lismullin centre – that's in Navan.'

She looked really excited. I can't say I was, although immediately I hoped it would be better than Rathmore. I knew it wasn't a course, I knew it wasn't special. They always said this when they wanted to move me. I got moved up and down from time to time, for a day here and there, sometimes back to Ballyglunin, but I was never told about it beforehand. The last time I'd been 'sent for training' I had ended up in Rathmore. I suspected I was going for good.

'You'll be there for a while,' she confirmed, 'so you can get the train to Ballyglunin first and pack all your things before you go up, okay?'

That seemed weird to me, since I'd been in Rathmore for months and didn't really have much to pack in Ballyglunin anyway. I wore a uniform here, and the directors had taken all my good stuff. But I looked forward to seeing the girls. I had missed them.

But Niamh and Mary Flanagan were the only girls there. Sharon and the others had left.

Then, word came to me that Miss Byrne, one of the residents of Ballyglunin had been in a car crash and had died. I knew Miss Byrne, she had been at so many of the get-togethers there. I couldn't stop crying, with the other girls too, but there was a sense of something dark about the reactions of the numeraries.

'Miss O'Rourke told me her wardrobe was a disgrace,' I heard Miss O'Reilly say, 'it's no surprise, her soul was clearly not spotless either.'

She shrugged as if the death was inevitable.

That frightened the shit out of me. If Miss Byrne was a target for the wrath of God, I hadn't a hope. I did extra penance and wore my cilice eagerly. It was easier with pop socks instead of tights, they only ripped when you wore them over it. I tightened it so that I would limp. This would keep me safe.

―――――

My dad called spontaneously. Usually I would get a message in Rathmore to tell me to call home, and I would phone the box. But as I passed the phone in Ballyglunin it rang. He seemed just as surprised as I was to connect directly with one another.

'Anne Marie, we are long overdue a visit,' he said. 'You haven't seen your mother in a long time. I want you to come home.'

I said I'd try.

'Ah, Anne Marie,' he said, 'that's what you always say – would you just come visit us, please? I'll ask Bernadette to come that weekend, and we can make sure everyone is here.'

It sounded lovely. Something tore at my heart, a brief homesickness that clutched at the normality of Ballyvourney and the Grand Hotel. Looking back, I know it was that I missed fun, but I told myself it was a demon trying to twist me. A devil inside me trying to take over.

'Your course comes first,' Dad added, 'but we haven't seen you, Anne Marie, you're our daughter ...' Then he added, 'Maybe I'll just come across with Mam and see you at your college instead ...'

'No, Dad, don't,' I said. 'I'll ask.'

I spoke to Miss Smith immediately. 'He said he wants to pop down,' I said.

'Maybe you should pop home for a bit,' she suggested straight away. 'Niamh is finishing with us in a few weekends, and it's arranged that her brother is collecting her, so maybe you could go then.' She thought about it. 'But we need to discuss the terms and all the bits and bobs with Miss Cathy.'

Miss O'Rourke wasn't so sure.

'What if they don't let you return?' she said.

'I'm 17,' I said. 'I'll just come back.'

My parents still didn't know I had signed up to Opus Dei. I knew they'd let me come back because they believed in this course, just like all of us had. I told her so.

'Right, but ...' Miss O'Rourke said, still suspicious, 'you see ... this is the thing, people with the ... Devil in them ... they hate Opus Dei ...' her voice got excited and unsteady, 'and, well, they will try to poison you against us, so if they try to stop you coming back to us, scream and cry and run away. Okay?'

'Yes,' I said, 'I'll just scream and scream.'

Miss O'Rourke breathed in and out as if to calm herself at the thought of it. 'Do you know our number off by heart?'

I did.

She lectured me heavily before I went home, with Miss Smith and Miss Diaz, in a get-together in her room, just the four of us.

'Now listen,' she said, 'when you go back you can perhaps give them the idea that you might be thinking of joining us.'

'But I have joined?' I reminded Cathy. I was already over a year in the Work.

'I know,' Miss O'Rourke said, 'but you don't want to hurt them, and you are nearly 18 now, it's your life, so maybe just let them know now.'

Miss Smith agreed, and so did Miss Diaz. Now was the time to hint at my new life.

'They'd be hurt if they knew you whistled already.' Miss O'Rourke was sure.

'We don't need to hurt them,' Miss Diaz said, 'if you hint, give them an idea, then they will gradually accept it. I will pray on this later, Anne Marie, and it will all be all right.'

On the way by later I could hear yelps coming from Miss Diaz's room and the sound of lashes on top of lashes. I ran down the steps and blocked my ears.

———

Niamh Moore's brother Steve drove up for her as she finished up in Ballyglunin. I sat on her bed as she packed and I felt wretched. I couldn't believe she was leaving.

'New girls will be starting with us,' Miss Smith said when I expressed myself, 'more suitable girls.'

Whatever that meant.

Niamh swung out of her brother in a bear hug when she saw him, even though she went home all the time. Steve was a nice guy, I'd known him for years, and he was going with a girl from my class for a long time. Niamh was dying for them to get married, she always went on about it.

'You'd be at the wedding,' she used to say, 'we would have such a laugh.'

Steve nodded at me as soon as he saw me and said, 'Anne Marie, long time no see.'

That felt strange because there had been a time when I would cross paths with people every single day, people like Steve, who now I didn't see at all. I thought about Mr Murphy in the hotel, and my neighbour Maureen who was always in our house. I thought about the faces of all the folks of Ballyvourney and what they used to mean in my life. Now it was almost as if that meaning was gone.

The journey wasn't long but I found it hard.

A song came on and Niamh turned up the radio.

'It's Lionel Richie's new one,' Niamh told me. 'He is such a hunk.' I knew who she was talking about, but I pretended I didn't. Lust was a mortal sin.

Niamh turned in her seat and took my hand and jigged it up and down. It was like she was telling me, remember, remember, but I just let it go. She sat turned that way looking at me for a few moments before giving me a small wink and turning back around. Niamh Moore was a wonderful person, through and through. She always treated me with softness I have never forgotten.

The radio played in the car all the way home and the two siblings sang along. I didn't sing. I knew none of the songs.

Twenty-two

As Steve's car came over the hill and I spotted Ballyvourney finally, it looked cuter and quainter than I remembered, and greener. The streets looked adorable in the golden afternoon sun, and one or two people walking waved at the car.

Our house seemed smaller and cleaner too. The TV was on. The fire was lit.

Mam was the only one there. She reached out and rubbed my arm when she saw me. That was a lot for my mother: she never touched anyone much at all.

'Now,' was all she said, 'your room is still there for you.'

My room looked the same, but my bed looked huge compared to the small ones that Opus Dei preferred.

Dad came in from work. I could hear him come in and start on the tea but I didn't know how to come down the stairs. I felt like I couldn't face him with this lie all over me.

'Are you here at all, love?' he called up the stairs, and I popped my head around the door. 'Arra would you look at that now?' he said. 'I wouldn't know you.'

I came down the stairs, but we didn't hug; we just looked at each other for a bit.

'You're skinny,' he said, and then he looked at the broken skin on my hands. 'What's this?'

I covered my hands with my sleeves.

'Probably from all the washing of the veg,' he told himself.

'I think I'll go for a walk, Dad, maybe,' I said, and my dad fussed a bit, fixing his jacket on the hook and trying to look nonchalant.

It felt like I had my self, and then I had this other part, like this other part of my mind that thought over my self. My thoughts would go along – the regular ones – but then they would get covered over with new holy ones, the ones full of quotes and accusations. It was confusing and really stressful.

My self was pleased to be here and wanted to run down to Mr Murphy and get straight back in beside him to do the stuffing, but my new side, the Ballyglunin Anne Marie, she was afraid of everything, and worried about everything, and seeing the Devil in everyone and everything. I was a machine built up around my true self, and I was on high alert.

I walked along the main road and the fresh air felt like medicine. I stretched my arms out and wiggled my fingers. My body could rest tonight. I was excited about that. I told myself I might even sleep in, and then felt guilty about it and promised myself not to.

Then, as I was walking past my old school entrance, I stopped, because I could see there was a coach pulled up and teenagers were coming out and getting onto it. I stood back under the trees and watched. They were dressed up, in lovely dresses and suits.

I realised it was the debs.

Then I saw Dan Gallagher, more handsome than ever, dressed up in a black suit. He had a girl with him, wearing a purple silk dress down to her feet, and her hair was all piled on her head. He didn't see me. He wouldn't have recognised me anyway. He let the girl go first onto the bus and I just stood there and watched her smile at him and say 'Thank you' and then they got on the bus. He took her hand and helped her up the steps.

Oh, did this girl take my future? That's how it felt at the time.

It felt as though, when Dan got on the bus, I lost everything, and I turned into the wall because of the gasps and cries that were coming out of me with the regret.

I wanted to be that girl, I wanted to wear a long purple dress and pile my hair up, and for my mother and my aunties to be in the house cooing over my choices and telling me I looked beautiful. I wanted my dad to walk me down to the school to meet Dan in a black suit and I wanted to go on the bus to my debs because I was only 17 and I was on my hands and knees scrubbing day in and day out for no one.

It felt like there was no one who knew me. I had no one.

I turned and fled, walking as fast as I could back to my house, in the door, past my dad and up the stairs into my old room and into my bed under the covers.

There was a knock on the door about ten minutes later.

'Anne Marie?' my dad called in.

'I'll be down in a minute,' I said, and I waited to hear him go down the stairs, and then I let go, into my pillow, with huge sobs that racked my shoulders and tore my throat and made my head nearly explode with the weight of all of this.

I couldn't stand being home. Facing that life, the future I had dreamed of so often, not specifically with Dan but with *someone*, and seeing it slip away so clearly like that, it felt like I had lost my life.

But counteracting that were internal accusations of lust and greed, and the worst sins you could do. Being home panicked me. Seeing Dan there and feeling the way I did about it, I believed in that moment that was the Devil trying to tempt me out of Opus Dei and into a life of badness and lust.

Opus Dei had warned me about this. They had told me what to do. The Devil was here in Ballyvourney. I was to be strong and fight for my vocation against the Devil, right here, right now. And I was scared out of my wits.

I wanted to go back to Ballyglunin.

Twenty-three

I was glad to see my mother up, glad to see her smile at me as I came down. You could always tell when Mam was having a good day or a bad one based on her smile.

We sat around our family table and ate plates of boiled potatoes with salt and butter, topped with mince and gravy. My brothers filled me in on school and the to-ings and fro-ings of our village. They talked over one another until my father told them to whisht and they shut up.

'You've been so busy, Anne Marie,' my mother said to me, 'I don't think I can remember the last time I talked with you at all.'

I did. Miss Smith had been listening in, standing right beside me.

'I really like living there,' I said, 'and learning everything, and being with everyone – it's a really special life.'

'When you qualify, now,' my mam said, and reached over me to get the butter, 'you'll be able to teach, right?'

I nodded and swallowed. She replaced the butter on the far side of me again.

She seemed so disordered doing that.

'You should just ask me to pass the butter,' I said.

She said she would the next time. Then my dad picked up

208

a whole potato on his fork, mashed it into the plate with the butter. It was terrible manners. I looked away.

'Behaviour is how we can show we love God,' I said in his direction.

Dad looked up.

'Ah.' He thought it over. 'I can see from living down there with that crowd – those well-to-do women – are they rubbing off at all, do you think?'

'That's not a bad thing,' I said. 'Opus Dei is doing wonderful things, and I am going to join the organisation myself' – I sniffed and pushed food around the plate – 'by the way.'

My dad dropped the smile. He stared at me and then he looked at my mother and pushed his chair back. His fork went down, his hands went into fists and he rested them on the edge of the table.

'Now listen to me,' he said. 'Now, Anne Marie … no, that is not happening at all.'

'Yes it is,' I said. 'I am going to join Opus Dei. I want to.'

My parents looked at each other again.

'And never come home from the Holy Joes?' one of my brothers asked. My dad put a warning finger up to him.

'I want to join Opus Dei,' I said. 'God has chosen me to follow my vocation.'

'What are you telling me? A vocation? Would you ever …' He laughed out loud and his fists turned into two flat hands on the table. 'Bernadette will not stand for this,' he said, patting his hands against the wood. 'Go out there to that phone now,' he told me, shaking his head, 'and ring your aunt up and say that to her and see—'

I pushed my chair back. 'I am going to join – it doesn't matter what Bernadette says.'

'You will not!' Dad said.

I picked up my plate, and washed it and put it away before I left the kitchen, going upstairs and into my bed, pulling the covers up around me. Nobody followed me up, but I could hear my father ranting in the kitchen.

This was not my life; my real life was in Ballyglunin. It was safer there.

Being home, without the rhythm of the quotes, the parroting of Josemaría Escrivá at every opportunity, I felt really unbalanced, like I couldn't focus. How could I focus when I didn't know what was going to happen next? How could I focus when I didn't know what people were going to do?

I repeated sayings and prayers quietly under my breath. None of them made much sense, but they calmed me down.

My dad knocked on the door of my room later. Then he opened it, and stood there for a moment, looking back down the stairs a few times before he said anything.

'Mr Murphy there in the Grand …' he began, not really looking at me. 'Well, some of your old gang, and Tony, are working there – you got that in the letter I sent, right?'

I nodded, but no, I hadn't got a letter.

'I was up there just now myself,' Dad said, 'and Mr Murphy and I got talking, well, I told him you were back for a trip and he asked me if there was any way we could spare you as they have some do on and not enough people.'

I started to say no.

'And, well,' Dad continued, 'I promised him you would.'

'Would? Would what?'

'Work the week out for him. He was delighted when I said you would, said he has never found a girl like you again.'

I don't know what emotion I felt when Dad said that. A dizzy mix of pleased and horrified.

'Dad, I ...'

'Now, Anne Marie,' Dad said, 'the man asked and I answered and I promised him you would, so you will.'

I don't know what I had thought I would be doing for the week, but I had never thought of working back in my old job, not even for a second.

———

'Well, well, would you look?' was all Mr Murphy said to me when I came into the hotel kitchen the following morning.

Walking down there I had felt like I was walking to certain doom. And when I went in, and everyone acted like that was normal – for me to be there – it felt surreal. Nothing much had changed in the years since I had left home. Everything looked smaller now, though, and there was too much furniture and too much pattern.

But all the same, as soon as I got into the kitchen, I went straight to it, with a wink from Carrie, who was at the sink washing trays and handed me a tea towel to get drying.

'We feel like you've been gone years,' she said.

'I have been,' I said.

'Got yourself a fella in Galway, I bet?' Carrie said, and the inference mortified me, sent me scuttling back into my brainwashed persona.

I shook my head. 'I have not!' I wanted to bless myself but I just dried the dishes.

Mr Murphy called my surname and I went over to where he was, as always, at the prep station. He didn't give me a welcome or even a hello, but I could see he was pleased to see me. He looked sideways at me.

'Separate those legs from the bird there.' He had a knife in one hand and was holding three carrots with the other, chopping them fast as he spoke. He didn't even look up. Beside him were five turkeys, all roasted and glistening in their silver trays.

'The legs?' My heart sank.

'The legs,' he affirmed, and pointed with his knife at the carcasses.

The thing was, I didn't know how to do it, although I had seen Mr Murphy do it many times as if it was second nature. Maybe I could bluff it.

I picked up a knife and attempted it, pulling the leg away from the body and pushing the blade in where the join was. Clear juice spurted out and meat fell, but the bone stayed attached. I shoved the knife downward onto it. It had no effect.

Mr Murphy put down his knife. 'Wrong knife,' he said.

I put down the one I had.

'That's a vegetable knife,' he told me, pronouncing every consonant, and handed me a large knife from the rack.

I attempted the leg again.

'I thought you were at the end of your second year into training as a chef, Anne Marie ...' Mr Murphy said, matter-of-factly, over his glasses. It wasn't a question.

'They haven't taught us this yet,' I said.

'I see,' he said. 'Just on the salads still, are you? Learning how to chop the carrots and the potatoes, how to peel spuds, is it? Or is that too advanced after two years?'

I stared at him. We never had roast turkey in Ballyglunin, or even chickens; we always made things with chopped-up meat or just plain steaks or chicken breasts.

'You know how to slice meat, at least?' he said, and I did this half-nod and a look of indignance. 'If so, get going on that. Turkey breast, slice it.'

My face clearly fell, because I could see he was really disappointed. He tutted under his breath. Then he pushed another knife toward me, and a two-pronged fork. I knew the use for neither. But I stuck the fork into the turkey anyway, and dragged the knife across the meat, cutting into it. The knife seemed dull and I dragged meat into lumps instead of slices.

'For the love of God,' he said, exasperated, grabbing the implements and pushing me gently out of the way. 'Stop hacking it, it's this way, *with* the meat, not against it.'

When he cut, the meat sliced with no effort.

'You don't know how to do it, do you?' he asked as he continued. I knew that turkey didn't even need to be sliced; I knew he was just proving the point he had to make, that he had told me so.

I left the kitchen, took my apron off and handed it to Carrie on my way out the door. I could not stand this embarrassment. I knew I was not being taught anything. Maybe I didn't need it. I had God and I had Opus Dei. I was worthwhile in the

213

organisation, I was needed. Opus Dei needed me. Jesus and God loved me.

There were answers in Ballyglunin. I was wanted in Ballyglunin. That was something I knew. I had a vocation as big as a house.

———

When my dad came home from work, he knew all about it. 'You left the job?'

'Yep,' I said.

'They said they won't pay you.'

'I don't need that money,' I said. 'I don't need that job. I am going home soon.'

He looked like he had been stung when I said that.

'This is your home, Anne Marie,' he told me.

But it didn't feel like home any more. It felt difficult and upsetting, like I was on the run from something. I had a constant knot in my stomach. People were asking me things instead of telling me things, and I missed my routine.

It was like my body didn't know how to live if I wasn't working hard. I started cleaning my family home from top to bottom, spending so much time on my knees scrubbing and scrubbing for no good reason that my knees bruised. I offered it up for God. I pinched myself and pulled the hair on my legs through my skirt. I went to bed and prayed until my mouth was moving on its own. I needed to be where that was normal. I wanted to go back. I wanted to be where I didn't have to think.

I wanted to go back.

That night was the night of the Stardust fire. I remember staring at the television as the news was read and feeling so sick. Everyone who was killed there was my age.

I couldn't sleep a wink.

The following day I spent the morning walking around and around the village, saying the rosary over and over.

When I saw Mr Murphy dragging the huge bin bags out to the back of the hotel, I turned around and walked the other way. I went straight to a phonebox and rang Ballyglunin and asked to be collected and brought home.

Miss Smith came for me straight away.

On the way back to Ballyglunin she asked me if I had heard about the Stardust.

'I saw it on the news,' I said, as sadly as I felt.

'Young people who dance with the Devil ...' she said, nonchalantly, emphasis on *dance*, as she changed gear, 'cannot be surprised when they burn in hellfire ...'

Then she did a little *tch* sound with her tongue, the way you would if you spilled a drop of milk. She turned the wipers on. 'Will this weather ever make its mind up?' she said.

It took me a minute to put those words in the right order, because when she said them my mind went into overdrive.

I realised what Miss Smith was insinuating: that the Devil had caused Stardust.

I didn't realise until years later that the Devil was the one driving the car I was sitting in.

Twenty-four

M y parents were up the walls.

Cardinal Basil Hume in England had written a letter about Opus Dei and it was all over the papers. It was Christmas 1981.

'For a considerable time I have studied carefully certain public criticisms made about the activities of Opus Dei in Britain and I have also examined the correspondence addressed to me on the same subject ...' the letter began.

And there was a line in it that had really upset my father: he went over and over it on the phone.

'No person under 18 years of age should be allowed to take any vow or long-term commitment in association with Opus Dei ... young people who wish to join Opus Dei should first discuss the matter with their parents or legal guardians.'

My dad had sent me a cutout from the newspaper. He was calling all the time.

'Anne Marie,' he said, 'I am not happy at all about this now, and you're barely replying to our letters!'

I had accidentally answered the phone when it rang as I was passing by. Usually a numerary would have got to the phone before us assistant numeraries.

'I'm busy, Dad,' I said.

My dad was very stressed.

'Niamh applied to every single hotel in Cork,' he told me. 'That so-called diploma she got there in that so-called college was not worth a thing, not a thing.'

I said nothing, but my stomach dropped when he said that. I knew Niamh had been counting on that diploma to find work. I also knew my diploma, not that I'd been given it yet, was equally worthless. I was telling my family I was doing extra courses, so they would be placated and not expect me home.

'Anne Marie,' my dad asked then, in a whisper, 'how far in are you with these people? Exactly what vows have you taken?'

He said hello to someone then, someone passing. I knew he would be standing half in and half out of the phone box in the village. I knew the way he would be standing as well, hand on the frame of the box, leaning with the phone to his ear. I'd stood there with him myself so many times as he rang up to his sisters or his brothers above.

'Anne Marie,' he said, 'are you being kept there?'

'No,' I said.

'Are you going to come home again?'

I could not answer him. I didn't know. I didn't want to.

'Not at all,' he said. 'I think you're being prevented. This thing I read, we all read, about Opus Dei.'

'It's not true,' I told him.

'It is so,' he said, and I could hear the sound of the paper he clearly had in his hand.

'It isn't true, Dad,' I said, 'you have it wrong.'

The directors had given us the information we needed to handle this.

'I understand the commotion,' Miss O'Rourke said. 'We have read the directive ourselves and it's very clear.' She cleared her throat and read from a page: '"If there are, by exception, good reasons for not approaching their families, these reasons should, in every case, be discussed with the local bishop or his delegate." What that means is that we should have guidance, and girls, we do already. We have priests and the bishop himself to speak to on these matters, always have done, always will.'

My dad wasn't having that. 'Are you being prevented from writing to us?' he asked me again.

He didn't have a clue. Nobody was stopping me doing anything, let alone putting any pen to any paper.

'I have to go,' I said.

'You have to go, you have to go – that's the only thing you've told me about yourself since you left this house, Anne Marie. What have you been up to? What kind of things are they getting you to do?'

I didn't answer.

I didn't tell him that, a few weeks before, Opus Dei had confirmed my vows of poverty, chastity and obedience in a ceremony called the oblation that was sprung on me without explanation. I had been told of it in the morning, and by the afternoon it had been done. Being double bound came with extra privileges, Miss Smith told me in excited tones. I would now be allowed handle the chalice in the oratory, but only with a linen cloth.

I had hesitated when Miss O'Rourke took me to practise the vows.

'I already made a commitment in Rome,' I pointed out.

When that didn't put her off, I stalled again.

'My dad is really upset,' I said.

'Anne Marie,' Miss O'Rourke said, 'priests have taken the afternoon away from their work for this. Do you want to waste their time?'

I shook my head. 'No.'

'You did make your commitment in Rome already, Anne Marie. This day isn't serious at all; in fact, we just do the second time as a way of keeping the bishop happy.'

So I believed her and said the words out loud in front of witnesses. I made those vows. But I didn't want to tell my father that.

'Can I come for a visit?' he said then. 'I could drive across and get us some lunch.'

'I don't have time for that, Dad,' I said, not wanting to tell him that a) I was back in Rathmore, and b) even if he did come to Dublin I was not allowed go out for lunch.

I was up and down to Dublin all the time, being put to good use in the centres there and in other ones around Ireland. It made no odds to me; at least the journey gave me a small rest, because the rest of the time I was worked to the bone.

'You are not to join that organisation without seeing us,' he told me.

'Maybe I already did, Dad!' I said.

There was a gasp. He said nothing.

'Bye, Dad.' I hung up.

I turned from the phone to see Miss Diaz standing there.

'What were you saying there?' she asked, eyeing me. Her

tongue lisped over the S sounds of her second language.

'Nothing,' I said.

'Was your father talking about the directive?' she asked. 'Was your father giving out about Opus Dei?'

I nodded.

'And you let him?' Her eyes flashed at me.

'He was a bit worked up,' I explained, but she seemed really annoyed.

'I think *you* should be ashamed,' she said with a snarl, 'not standing up for your vocation and your Opus Dei family. Are you going to curl up like a little kitten, Anne Marie, any time your vocation is challenged? Is that what our Father did in his lifetime? Is that what the Lord Himself did? No. It's wrong to allow the Work to be disparaged. You need to fight for your vocation and your Opus Dei family, Anne Marie.'

It was as if my whole body went into pins and needles.

Later I went into the bathroom after Miss Diaz and there was a smell of burning. I never did find out what that was, but it wasn't the first time – not in Ballyglunin or any Opus Dei centre – that I smelled that burning. And once, in Gort Ard, in the men's bathrooms when I was cleaning I saw matches and a candle.

As I passed her in the hallway, her coming out and me going in, I noticed a strong smell.

A few days later I was sent back to Rathmore. I cried all the way there.

———

My dad must have written to me that same night. A few weeks later I got the letter, and it was well worn. It would have arrived in the afternoon post to Ballyglunin, read, read again, sent up, and it arrived to me about a week later in Dublin. The numeraries liked to make sure there was nothing sinful in our post. When it finally got clearance, Miss Duffy called me to read out a censored version. I could see the strike throughs as the light shone through the paper.

'Everything is good at home,' Miss Duffy read it out, 'your brother is doing well at the hurling, and Maureen next door got new windows.'

She was a creepy woman who smiled all the time like a Cheshire Cat, and who would sit too close and make this weird humming sound back at me when I spoke. I imagined she was actually a glitching robot, caught on some internal whirr. I absolutely hated our *charlas* because of it, and because nothing I said was satisfactory to her. She always wanted more and more from me, asking me to explain things I had no explanation for.

'How are you really?' she would ask. 'Really?'

'I'm okay,' I said. 'Tired.'

'Oh? Tired?'

'Yeah.' I regretted every word I spoke, because it was all taken so seriously.

'Tired why?' she asked.

I shrugged, no real ideas coming to mind except for working so hard.

'Work,' I said, matter-of-fact.

'Hmmm.' She nodded and then repeated the word: 'Work …

why do *you* really think you are tired, Anne Marie?'

These conversations made me feel stressed and invaded. So I just shrugged. It was pointless talking to this one, to any of them. They just spoke in riddles or responded to my questions with questions.

'What is it that you want, Anne Marie?' she said then, almost as if she was irritated, in a tone that teachers or parents use when a child won't let up. I had used that tone myself with my brothers.

It was a strange question. She had never asked me that before and I don't think she even meant to ask it, or start this chain reaction.

I wanted something *more*, something different. I knew that for sure now. But I was confused. What did I want? I settled for a while on the idea of a hobby, and maybe going outside of Opus Dei to get a certificate or something.

'A night class?' Miss Duffy said in response to me bringing it up. I had asked three times now, each time reacted to as if it was the first, each time reacted to as if it was a bananas thing to enquire after.

'A night class in what?' she asked.

'Something,' I said, 'anything.'

'Something,' she repeated, 'anything ... well, that's not very specific.'

To be honest, I am sure I was subconsciously thinking of the outside world – of going back to Ballyvourney with my tail between my legs. If I learned something, at least I could say I had done that.

'English or something,' I suggested.

'Everything you need to learn is provided here.' Miss Duffy was done with the conversation. She stood up, dusted off her skirt and started to act busy, looking around the room for something. She didn't say what.

'Where is my ...' she began, and opened the door and went out of the room, leaving me standing there.

I was glad, though, as I had to get back to the kitchen. I had floors to scrub and then, after that, an entire floor of windows to clean. Normally in these *charlas* I said what I had to in order to get through and get back. Nobody was doing my chores while I was in there, so they piled up and made me late.

I was dealing with very heavy periods and awful gastric issues. My skin was bad with acne and rashes. My knees and hips and back hurt from hard work. I had ulcers in my nose and mouth that wouldn't go away. I had warts all over my hands. So, out of habit at this stage, I complained a lot.

But the doctor was never called.

'You know, Anne Marie,' Miss Duffy had said to me, 'temptation attacks the body and eats you up.' Numeraries were obsessed with the idea of temptation. 'You must not give in. Prayer will be your salvation.'

It was not temptation. By now I was far too tired and sick to ever so much as daydream. My problems stemmed from a lack of fresh air, a lack of sleep and the constant work and pressure. I was, as an assistant numerary, eating leftovers every day. I was being suppressed and oppressed, and it was affecting me physically.

'Why do *you* believe you feel tired, Anne Marie?' she asked again, giving me a long look.

I shrugged again.

'Have you had impure thoughts at night?' she asked. 'Are you allowing temptation to take over?'

I know I wrinkled my face up. What on earth was she even talking about? This was not a conversation I wanted to have with Miss Duffy. But it was a conversation that I kept being dragged into. I knew why, as well.

Twenty-five

There was a lot of drama in Opus Dei since the directive.

A car had pulled up outside the conference centre in Lismullin the morning after the directive was published. I had been working up there on the 'special course' that was nothing except being shown exactly how they liked that place scrubbed and then set to do it.

The parents of an assistant numerary called Jane were in it, and they arrived accompanied by two nuns – both with faces of absolute fury – and the four of them walked straight in to get Jane, going through the front entrance of the centre, with such a sturdiness and deliberateness that nobody said a thing. Not one word. They walked into the room we were wiping down, and Jane just put her cloth down and sighed. She said nothing either. She just followed them out.

'Start crying and run after the car!' the directress shouted, as it drove down the driveway. And all the other assistant numeraries, did, screaming, 'Jane! Jane!' and making a show. I ran after them a little, but I didn't scream at first, because I didn't know Jane that well and I was frightened by it all. I was also totally confused by it. This heroic display that only started after the car had moved off, it seemed weird and pointless. Why hadn't they stopped her parents in person? Who was this performance for? To this day I have no idea, but almost caught up in the hysterics, I suddenly found myself joining in and running down the road, screaming and crying out for Jane as if I'd known her all my life.

Then we lost Maureen Carroll, Meg we called her, from Tipp. She was such a dote, a really gentle girl. We shared a room with another girl. Maureen's brother was getting married. She was told she couldn't go, she whispered to me after we went to bed.

'They said I wasn't to,' she said, and I saw tears in her eyes in the dark. Little glimmers and rivulets on her skin.

'That's awful,' I said. 'Why did they say no?'

'They said that Irish weddings were full of temptation,' she said. Her eyes were fixed on me in the dark as if I could change things.

'They said that?' I thought about my mother's cousin's wedding and how much fun we had. Was that sinful? Maybe it was. One of the guests got really drunk at that. People were dancing like mad as well. But the priest was there at that. And weddings were in churches, weren't they?

'Wouldn't a priest be at it?' I asked.

Meg nodded. 'Of course – my two uncles and the parish priest.'

I stared back at her in the dark.

'Maybe pray about it, Meg,' I said.

The next day in the kitchen she didn't appear, and then later she didn't come to dinner. She came to work the next day, and I thought she was fine, but then after lunch she didn't appear, and when I went up to the toilet after dinner I saw she was sitting on her bed.

'Are you sick?' I asked.

Meg went on like that – absent and distant – for a while, and then one morning I woke up and her bed was stripped and she wasn't in the bedroom. When I was getting dressed I saw her wardrobe was empty.

'Meg's gone,' I whispered to the rest. I looked at her empty chair in the dining room and missed her so much.

The girls whispered in the kitchen. 'She left late last night, middle of the night, her brother collected her.'

The directors told us not to speak of Meg, ordered us in the get-together to forget her for good and never to mention her name.

'Terrible things happen to those who turn away from their vocation,' Miss O'Rourke said. 'Hellish things, Hell on earth. When you are sent a vocation and you put your hand up to God's loving face and say no, and refuse His gift to you ... that is the Devil inside of you taking over, and you will burn in Hell. All we can do,' Miss O'Rourke sighed, 'is pray.'

We said a decade of the rosary as if Meg was dead.

'Are you thinking about boys?' Miss Duffy asked me now, grinning like a clown.

I shook my head and stood up.

'I have to get going,' I said. 'I've a lot to do. I'm not thinking about anything.'

We lost another girl, Rose, the same way as Meg, not long after she went home for a visit. When she came back she was different.

'I went to the hop,' she told me with bright eyes. 'I shouldn't have ... of course ... Miss Duffy has told me it was a mortal sin' – her voice lowered – 'but my sister was egging me on and I didn't know the harm ... I've been making it up to God since, I swear, and I've been to Confession every day.'

As the weeks wore on, Rose seemed more and more eager to make peace with God. She started sleeping on the floor every night and I could hear her whipping herself in the bathroom.

'She danced with some fella,' Pat told me, as we teamed up to fold the underpants for the male numeraries in the laundry. Rose usually did it, but these days she was constantly in with her spiritual director.

'I know,' I said, 'she told me.'

This was a job I hated doing, even more so than washing underpants. Washing them was easy: they came to us in bags with their names embroidered on each bag, and we just dumped those all together and fecked them into the machine. We did the same into the dryer. But folding them, individually, into piles for each person – it made me feel like the lowest of the low.

I remembered Rose's comment the first time we did the folding together.

'We're wives,' she had said, 'without the benefits!'

I'd thought she was being dirty and crude then, so I'd ignored her. And I had told on her to my spiritual director, Miss Duffy, because I had nothing else to say. She'd told me to give Rose a fraternal correction, saying that her comment could cause impure thoughts.

When I did, Rose had looked at me and said, 'Thank you, Anne Marie.'

But now Rose was doing morning Mass on her knees on the hard floor, and keeping silence until well after breakfast, and I noticed her limp from the cilice on her leg when she was cleaning.

One time I saw her scratching her arms. They were bright red.

'Rose, is everything okay?' I asked, but she didn't answer.

Kate Boyle leaned in as we were working and spoke out of the side of her mouth. 'She got a letter the other day.'

'From who?' I wanted all the information. Rose wasn't herself at all.

'The man she danced with,' Kate told me, 'asking her to go with him. He said he wanted to see her again.'

I went straight to Rose. My thoughts on it were that she shouldn't reply. She had to ignore it. Of course, now I know that my panic was half for Rose and half for myself. Because I was desperate for her to stay. If she left that meant we had choices. If Rose went away to be with a man, like Meg did, we had free will and we could choose our own life.

I didn't want that to be true.

'Did you get a letter from a man?' I asked straight out when I saw her.

'They ripped it up,' she said, 'don't worry, and ...' she closed her eyes for a moment, 'I've been praying very hard about it.'

It wasn't enough information.

'Can you write back?' I asked.

'No.' She shook her head violently. 'I do not want to.'

But she did. It was so obvious she did. Everything about Rose changed, as she crucified herself to try to reverse the natural humanity inside of her.

I walked into the bedroom one evening and saw her spraying her arms with deodorant. She was hissing air through her teeth and I realised she was spraying the deodorant onto cuts she had made on her skin. When she saw me she threw the can onto the bed and refused to say anything about it. I knew what she was doing was wrong. We were not supposed to do things without asking, even for the sake of suffering or mortification.

'If I feel like I should mortify myself,' I said to Miss Duffy once, 'why do I have to ask?'

'For the cilice and whip you should always let me know,' she said.

'And what about other things?'

'Like what?'

I gave in. 'It's just that Rose is doing a lot of penance.' I was genuinely worried.

'Like what?' Miss Duffy hunched forward with a pained expression that did not look sincere.

'All sorts,' I said. 'She is kneeling a lot in the oratory, and she isn't covering her cuts when she cleans.'

I didn't tell her about the spray.

'Rose can come to talk to me if she wants,' Miss Duffy said. 'Other people's spiritual lives are not your business, Anne Marie.'

That was a giant contradiction. I was supposed to correct people all the time.

'It's just that if someone was hurting themselves too much ...' I paused then.

'Loved be pain,' Miss Duffy said. 'Glorified be pain.'

I knew those quotes; they were the Founder's. They said them all the time. But that wasn't my question.

'No,' I prodded, 'I mean if I feel that I want to do a mortification, why do I have to ask?'

'Do you want to use the whip?' Miss Duffy asked.

'No,' I said, 'it's just a question – do I have to ask?'

'If you want to use the whip or cilice outside of our times,' she told me, a little impatiently, 'you must ask me, as your spiritual directress, and I can give you permission.'

'But anything else is up to me?'

'I suppose it is,' she said.

I stared at her.

'Blessed be the pain,' she said. I knew that quote too.

A week later, very early one morning, Rose left Opus Dei and never came back.

———

Catherine came into the kitchen one day in great form.

'They're letting us watch the match,' she said.

'There is no way,' I said, almost holding onto myself with the excitement. It was the All-Ireland Final, and Cork were playing Kilkenny. I'd never have imagined for a second that I'd get to see it, I never got to see any sport at all.

'Miss Duffy is from Kilkenny,' Catherine said, 'they're putting it on the television upstairs.'

I punched the air half-heartedly and gave her a little smile. 'I'll believe it when I see it,' I said.

I worked extra hard that day, determined to give nobody any excuse to delay me. Then I went upstairs and into the TV room.

I nodded to the cross and blessed myself but even when we had the television on and the room was crowded with numeraries and assistant numeraries, sitting on the couches and on the floor, I still didn't believe I could be this lucky.

I felt a stir of my old self, tapping the floor with my foot as Ray Cummins, strong legs under him, flew up the pitch and scored a point for Cork.

But it wasn't really until the second part of the match, when the tribal instincts took me over and I could feel the pulse of my own heartbeat as the red players of Cork, my county, battled against Kilkenny, that I really relaxed and took it in. Kilkenny were in the lead, but Cork man Pat Horgan had the ball.

I sat forward. I could feel the thrill of the match, the tribal sense taking over me and pushing me forward in my seat and clutching at my chest with adrenaline.

Miss Duffy sat forward too.

'Come on, Cork!' I yelled to the telly, catching myself halfway and calming it down. It was hard to resist shouting, these games between such old rivals were so fun. Miss Duffy looked over. Herself and the other numeraries were watching quietly, Miss Duffy would smile now and again and nod if her lads got the ball. I, however, had at this point now a hold of Catherine by the leg and I was starting to get so engrossed in the play that I was forgetting my own goodness altogether.

'Jesus!' I squealed when our side lost the ball all of a sudden.

Then Kilkenny had it again, and they were tearing up the pitch. I couldn't contain myself. I could barely breathe. I stood up and my hands went into fists above my head. I shook them.

'Anne Marie,' Miss Duffy said.

I punched upward, turned to her with wide eyes, back to the TV.

'Jesus! Come on!' I yelled. I jumped on my feet.

'Anne Marie,' Miss Duffy said again. I heard her both times but it was like I couldn't turn my head. I shouted, 'Come on, Cork!'

'Anne Marie,' Catherine said, pulling my sleeve. 'Sit down!'

I clapped a hand over my mouth, our lads were after the ball again, back from the far side. My hands went up in the air and I went up on my tiptoes.

'Get it!' I roared. 'Get the FUCKING BALL!!!'

It was a fierce battle of a match but Kilkenny were just too strong on the day. Cork lost it and I wished more than anything I was in the lobby of the Grand Hotel with my brothers and my parents, running over the mistakes made, how we could have done better, willing things to have been different.

'Anne Marie.' Miss Duffy was by the door, frowning.

I went out.

'We are representing God in this moment, Anne Marie,' she said, 'you behaved like an animal inside of that room.'

'I—'

'As a member of Opus Dei,' she told me, 'we are striving to be saints, you are striving to be a saint, a canonisable saint, not a hooligan, not an animal.'

'I'm sorry,' I said, 'Cork—'

'That behaviour is sinful,' Miss Duffy said.

I nodded. My cheeks burned and I wanted to go off by myself. She lectured me for another while before she let me go. I went upstairs to my room and opened the window to cool my face.

I wanted to go home.

Twenty-six

I had nothing of my own, no money and no clothes except my uniform, and one outfit of a hand-me-down purple kilt and a jumper with a blouse that I could wear on special occasions, or for recruiting on public transport.

I was still asking for new shoes. I had been wearing the same shoes since I arrived in Ballyglunin nearly three years before.

I asked Miss Duffy in Rathmore, and Miss Smith and Miss O'Rourke in Ballyglunin. I asked Miss De La Luz too over and over again.

'Anne Marie,' she said, 'Opus Dei does not have money to spend on new shoes for everyone and anyone.'

'But …' I said, and showed her the state of mine, 'they're killing me, Miss.'

'They don't kill you,' she said, 'but let us believe that I am here to speak to you as spiritual director in place of God, and His direction through me today, I am sure, is to tell you to suffer this pain, like Jesus suffered the nails in His feet on the cross, and offer your suffering up to God.'

Was she serious?

'The answer to this problem, Anne Marie,' she said, 'is that you must love this agony, like Jesus did, and give yourself to God.'

This made no sense at all. I was starting to get so sick of this. More and more I was thinking about my family. My parents had issues, but they would never have let me walk around in these shoes. There was no way. The minute my mother noticed a too-small shoe you'd be rolled onto the bus to Macroom to get a new pair. They were never the ones you wanted, never the fashion, but I wouldn't care now.

'God speaks through me, Anne Marie,' Miss De La Luz said solemnly, and then she smiled and patted my shoulder and showed me the door back into the Administration, where piles of work were waiting for me.

Assistant numeraries were not paid, and so could never buy anything for themselves. We had to ask for everything, even small things. Everything was watched and counted, and if you had a special request it would be mulled over like you were asking for a loan of thousands and usually denied: even things like hairclips were major asks.

In contrast, the numeraries had full wardrobes filled with lovely modern clothes. I knew they did, because I cleaned their bedrooms. I used to open up their wardrobes and look at their fancy clothes from brands such as Laura Ashley and Esprit.

I remember once telling Miss O'Reilly that I loved the way Princess Diana had her hair, I said I might get the same.

'You need to go to Confession,' she said, really confusing me, 'you're materialistic.'

But *she* got new clothes after a shopping trip to Dublin once, and *she* even did a little fashion show for the assistant numeraries. That is how entitled and divided from us they were. I stood in my patched and glued shoes, watching her as she swished past in another expensive outfit she had bought, she said, in Arnotts.

'Where does all the money go?' I asked a numerary, a Miss Thomas, as we watched Miss O'Reilly twirl.

'Excuse me?' she said.

'The money we collect,' I said, 'where does it go?' I thought I knew: I was pretty sure it went to Arnotts.

A look of surprise crossed Miss Thomas's face, just a flinch of it, before her expression hardened and her eyes flashed and narrowed at me. Then she pulled me into the corridor and closed the door, trapping us outside.

She turned on me.

'If you ever say something like that again,' she said, whispering really close to my face, 'you'll go straight to Hell and so will your family.'

'Maybe that wouldn't be so bad,' I said in defiance under my breath as I left her. 'At least it would be warm.'

———

'There is a visitor for you, Anne Marie,' someone announced. I was in the Lisdara centre, cleaning on my knees in the dining room, and I stood up and looked at her like she had ten heads.

It was 1982 and I had been in Opus Dei now around four years, cleaning and scrubbing the same few buildings for a few weeks at a time, trafficked around Ireland without anyone ever asking me what I wanted or where I wanted to be. My mind was blanked out. That's how it felt. Blanked and dull, with no imagination left. I used to live in daydreams; now I just lived in a monotonous hell. My health was terrible, and the last few weeks I had been constantly crying. I'd been told I was to go back to Rathmore, and I was dreading it.

'A visitor?' I put my cloth down and took off my apron and followed her upstairs to where, in a corridor, the main numeraries, Ryan, Thomas and De La Luz, were in a huddle. I had no idea who the visitor was or what was going on.

'Anne Marie,' Miss Duffy called in a whisper, 'come here.'

I stood with them. They all kept looking sideways at the closed door of the sitting room. My visitor must be in there.

'Anne Marie,' Miss Thomas said, 'the Bishop of Meath has arrived here unannounced and asked to see you.'

I looked at her, and then at the others. Was this a joke?

'Why would he—' I began, but Miss Duffy shook her head and silenced me with a finger.

'Ssshhh,' she said. 'Now, listen, I know you have been very upset, Anne Marie, and that you don't want to go back to Rathmore, so we have all decided to let you go back to Ballyglunin.'

That confused me. What had that to do with the bishop?

'Come here.' Miss Thomas pulled me into another room and the others came in behind me and shut the door. 'Now look, Anne Marie, we don't know this bishop—'

'I don't know this bishop,' I said hurriedly.

Then Miss De La Luz gripped my arm. 'This is the second bishop coming here because of you!'

'The second?' What on earth were they talking about? Was this even real life?

'Yes,' Miss Thomas admitted, 'Bishop Casey was sniffing

around as well, phoning and writing on behalf of your father.'

My dad had a connection to Bishop Casey: that's where this was coming from, I realised.

'Forget that.' Miss Thomas shoved in and turned me around. 'Anne Marie, you are not to say anything to the bishop here. Do you hear me? You protect the organisation.'

Miss Duffy took over. 'Yes, give him the bare minimum only. If he asks how you are, say "Good," if he asks if you are happy, say "Of course."'

I nodded.

'And say you are following your vocation as an assistant numerary.' She frowned and screwed up her face. 'Just imagine to yourself that the Father himself is listening, do you understand me?'

I didn't say anything.

'Do you hear me?' she asked.

'I do,' I said. My brain felt squeezed.

The numeraries flanked me on either side as we entered the room, and the bishop, who had been sitting, stood up and waved both of his hands at them.

'Ladies, there is no need for you to step away from your duties,' he said. 'I will visit with Anne Marie on her own.'

When he said that, I pulled myself up to stand really straight. I was sweating and shaking from head to toe. How could I pull this off on my own?

'With all due respect, Bishop McCormack,' Miss Duffy said, 'in our organisation men and women must always be chaperoned.'

The bishop's eyes went so big when she said that, and she

continued hurriedly, 'Of course, not to say that is in any way a direction of how you should visit, Bishop McCormack, just that Anne Marie is learning things around here, and we like to continue formalities.'

He looked pretty mad anyway, but he didn't argue. He just stood there until the women left the room backwards. They left the door open, as per protocol.

Then the bishop sat down.

'Sit, sit, Anne Marie,' he said, lifting a hand to direct me to the opposing chair. Then he leaned forward. 'I wanted to come here to see you.'

'Yes, Bishop McCormack,' I said.

Reflected in the window of the hall, I could see the three women were flattened against the wall outside, eavesdropping.

'Anne Marie,' the bishop said, completely serious and focused on my face, 'you have not been home to see your parents in a long, long time.'

I nodded.

'Why is that?' he asked.

I looked to the door.

'I'm very busy with the Work,' I said. 'This is my family now.'

'Your parents, and your community, are worried,' he said. 'You haven't seen them in a long while now, too long. Are you happy here?'

'I am,' I said, looking at the door.

'You are?' He tilted his head and squinted at me, like he was trying to read something far away. 'You are aware of the Fourth Commandment, "Honour thy father and thy mother."'

'I love my life here, Father, I love the Work, and I am happy here.'

I could feel the size of the lie in my throat as I spoke. I swallowed hard.

'Right, right,' he said, looking to the door too. 'Now, Anne Marie, I want you to tell me the truth, and remember you are speaking to a bishop now, do you hear me?'

He was getting a bit frustrated with the door open. I was too. I wanted to close it and whisper to him that I had only ever wanted to be a chef, I had only ever wanted to go to London.

Instead I nodded my head and told him, 'I am very happy.' My chest stung and I knew my rash was going into overdrive. It got so irritated with any small upset. I scratched my neck and I could feel the bumps along the skin there.

Then I had an idea to placate him.

'I'll be going home soon,' I said loudly. 'I have plans to visit my family next week.'

'You do?' The bishop looked surprised. 'Your father was very worried when we spoke – does he know about the plan?'

'It's a surprise,' I said, really loud again.

'Well,' the bishop looked annoyed, 'I have to say I am not happy with this visit at all, Anne Marie.' He pointed at my neck. 'This rash all over you – you look very unwell and very unhappy, and I will be telling your father exactly that.'

'No, I'm fine,' I said. 'I just have a cold and I have a vocation to Opus Dei.'

The bishop stood up. He waved his hands forward and back across himself as he crossed the room to leave it.

'I am not impressed with this place at all,' he said.

I stayed frozen where I was. I heard the women fawn up to the bishop as he stormed down the corridor past them and out the front door.

Miss Duffy and Miss Thomas flew into the room, looking flustered and smiling falsely.

'What did you say to him?' Miss Duffy was clearly restraining herself from grabbing me. She looked like she wanted to physically squeeze every bit of information out of me.

'Nothing,' I said. 'I didn't say anything!'

'Well, he seemed to be impressed with us,' Miss Thomas said, but she was really agitated, walking back and forth.

I knew she was making that up. I was beginning to see the Opus Dei approach: pretend all is well and lie about it regardless.

———

My dad's line he kept giving me on the phone about my mother not being great – it wasn't a line. My brother Tony confirmed it.

'Mam's not well,' he said. 'The place is falling apart. Would you not come back for a bit?'

You might think that would annoy a girl, but it only brought guilt. Being a girl in the eighties meant we were automatically looked on as the fallback housekeepers. Things have changed a bit since then, thank God, but it was considered my place and my mother's place, and if she wasn't up to it, it wasn't as if my dad or brothers would jump into action. When Tony told me that, I wondered if I *should* go home. The idea of my dad and brothers struggling hurt me.

I talked to Miss O'Reilly about it.

'Anne Marie,' she scolded, 'you are always complaining, you must be happy.'

'I'll try,' I promised, 'but I feel like maybe I could go home to help for a while.'

'You are needed here,' she said, and made to stand up, as if that was all that had to be said.

'I am needed at home,' I said. 'The bishop said so.'

She sat back down again. She didn't say anything, she just made that listening face I hated so much.

I said again, 'I do believe that my family needs me … maybe God wants me to go.'

Miss O'Reilly looked wistfully at me. 'Oh, Anne Marie,' she said, 'we are your family now. God wants you here.'

I said I understood. 'But maybe I could take a weekend,' I said, 'to help Daddy.'

'Daddy,' she said, 'that's a very babyish way to say it.'

'Dad,' I amended.

She tapped her finger against the table, rubbed her palm along the wood. 'I think the place for you is Rathmore,' she said, and my heart sank down to my toes. It was a threat.

'No,' I said, 'I can't go back to there, it's the worst place, please. I'll stay here.'

'You seem very unsure of what you want, Anne Marie,' she said. 'You want to leave here, then you don't.'

'Don't mind me,' I said, with a little giggle. I swung my legs like a little girl.

'Anne Marie, the truth is,' Miss O'Reilly said, and she spoke with real authority, 'your mother probably has not got long left; she will probably be dead soon. She is not something you will have to worry about for too much longer.'

When she said that, I jumped up in shock and flew out of the room, leaving her door open, and ran downstairs.

'You're spoiled, Anne Marie,' I could hear her laugh, 'and you will be going back to Rathmore next week!'

I pulled at the latch of the huge Georgian front door, which we barely used, and dragged it open, rushing through it into the cold air, and I kept going.

Adrenaline electrified me, I ran and ran, down the path to the orchard, and then I stopped suddenly.

We weren't supposed to go out of the gates of Lisdara alone.

As if a switch inside of me flipped, I became the robot again. I turned around and went back, into the kitchen, and took up some housework.

There was a picture of Our Lady over the altar in the oratory in Lisdara. I cleaned it every day, but that day as I cleaned, I stopped what I was doing and looked at her. She was so serene, with her lovely blonde hair and her blue cloak and her lovely little baby with his crown and his hand out making the Sign of the Cross. A large gold halo surrounded her head. There were stars on it.

I looked at it and then I burst out laughing.

This was all nonsense.

This was all absolute shit.

Opus Dei had it all wrong. God and the Devil were not out to control me at all; I felt sure of it in that moment. It felt like I had figured out the plot of a movie before everyone else and

I stood there in shock.

I still didn't know what was true, but I knew what was not. This organisation was bullshit.

There was a book in Lisdara about the Hill of Tara and Irish archaeology. We were not allowed to read books because we had so much work to do, but I had noticed it – this small book – in the bookshelves in the sitting room. Nobody ever read that one, and it was almost there by accident, missed in a clear-out. It just sat on its own under a glass bowl in the corner of a lower shelf. I only knew it was there because I cleaned that shelf all the time. The numeraries, who never cleaned, would have missed it.

I dropped what I was doing and ran to get it, and I found a corner where nobody would see me, and I sat down on the floor and started to read.

It was a moment of rebellion to read that book. My heart hammered and I breathed like I was running a race as I flew through the pages, reading all about the archaeology of Ireland.

I came to a passage about how they had found the skull of a Barbary ape in an Irish fort. It was in Navan. And that struck me. Was that not incredible – that over two thousand years ago the Irish might have been travelling to the African continent, or Africans to this tiny island?

I felt a pride stir in me, for my people, for this island and its beautiful history. I read on and came across passages about the gods of Ireland, and the gods and goddesses who were worshipped here. I read about the Little People, the tribe of tiny men who would cause trouble if the locals didn't pay heed to them.

244

I knew that kind of belief. I held one *myself*.

What was the difference between those Irish people long ago believing in fairies and me here in this place believing in something like God and the Devil?

Nothing. Just different names on the holy and the troublemakers. I thought about the people in faraway countries who had their own gods too, and even the Protestants that I'd seen in Monkstown filing in and out of their church. We were all just people on earth with ideas. How on earth could we know who was right among us? God had never showed His face to any of us.

When they gave me a date to return to Rathmore, I knew it was over. I couldn't live that life again.

I would tell them I wanted to go home to see my family. I would tell them.

Twenty-seven

I wanted to visit my family. I was just fobbed off and fobbed off and sent back to Rathmore anyway. So I kept asking.

'Anne Marie,' Miss Duffy said, 'we will look into it.' She was growing so sick and tired of the same conversation, but I wasn't letting up.

'You've been looking into it for weeks now,' I said, feeling brave. 'It's not a problem, I can sort it all – I'll just get on the train to Cork and then get the bus to Killarney. Ballyvourney is on the way there.' I had an idea. 'I could do some apostolate on the bus journey.'

Miss Duffy pretended to think about that. She wrote the words *train – Cork – bus – Killarney* on her paper in her Filofax.

'Let me look into it,' she said again.

The next time I asked I was given a final answer. 'Anne Marie, we have thought about it, but you've so much on, myself and Miss Duffy can do the visit for you.' Miss Thomas said that as if it was a favour being done.

'You'll go?' I didn't get the point of that at all. 'To visit my parents?'

'Yes,' Miss Duffy said, 'we will go, the two of us, and visit them on your behalf. We can discuss your vocation as well, and sort things out for you.' She changed the subject then. 'Now, what have you to do this evening now yourself?'

'I've to make almond paste for Battenbergs,' I said, trying to get my head around what she had told me, 'for the men's supper over the way.'

In the kitchen nothing was ready to do that. I knew I couldn't blame the other assistant numeraries; they were so tired. I knew they had forgotten or just thought someone else would do it. But now I would be late to bed again.

Miss O'Reilly came to the door of the kitchen and looked around it. 'Anne Marie,' she said, 'could you do me up a plate of sandwiches and some biscuits and some drinks for our evening supper?'

'I've loads to do,' I said, pulling out bowls and trays. I crossed the kitchen and opened the presses, taking down apricot jam and ground almonds, shoving tins aside, looking for icing sugar.

'Have we no almond essence?' I asked. I checked another press.

'Anne Marie,' Miss O'Reilly said again, 'you can do that later. Now would you mind preparing those sandwiches and biscuits?'

'I was sure we had almond essence,' I said.

'Anne Marie!' She stood like an army captain. 'Will you stop with your almond essence? If you don't have it, make it!'

I stopped and turned on her like a lawyer in a court. 'Make it? These need to be ready for the male numeraries' supper in two hours.'

'Anne Marie!' She raised her voice. 'I have ordered a plate of sandwiches and tea!'

I lost my patience and snapped, 'Can't you just do it yourself?!'

Then I backed up against the counter with the shock of my own outburst.

'I don't have time,' I said. But something started to bubble up inside.

'Sandwiches, Anne Marie,' she said, 'and TEA!' She shouted the last word.

I turned and lifted and banged down every single tin and tray off the countertop, the clatters of them echoing off the kitchen walls.

Miss O'Reilly put her hands over her ears. 'What on—' she began, and then straightened up. Her face went solemn. A fraternal correction was on the way, I knew it.

'I don't want it,' I said. 'I do not want to even hear it.'

'Anne Marie,' she began, pressing a hand to her throat, 'I am speaking to you as God here and—'

'SHUT UP!' I shouted at her. 'SHUT UP SHUT UP!'

Her mouth dropped open and she stepped backwards.

I grabbed my head. The pressure in it, the dizzy rage, I didn't want to think, I couldn't allow myself think. I slammed my palms against my skull over and over and then I opened my mouth and I screamed.

'FUCKKKK OFFF,' I wailed.

My hands kept on slamming against my head over and over.

Miss O'Reilly ran. She took the stairs two at a time and I was shook into silence at the sight of her fleeing from me.

So I turned and ran into the storeroom, which was a tiny little square of the kitchen that had been panelled out to stock shelves full of tins and cookbooks and linen, swinging the door of it open as I grabbed the key out of it. I got in and locked the door from the inside.

Then I sat down on the floor.

Footsteps thumped down the stairs and across the kitchen floor.

I heard Miss Duffy's voice. 'She isn't here.'

A shuffle and another whisper: 'Where is she?'

The door of the pantry was jiggled. 'Anne Marie,' a voice said through it. Miss Duffy.

'Go away,' I said.

Then Miss O'Reilly, insisting that I unlock the door.

'No!' I started to cry, and with every jiggle of the door and demand to open it I got louder and louder, until I was actually keening in that old Irish way, with long wails like a baby who had hurt itself would, loud and cathartic.

The pins and needles came again, head to toe.

'Stop that! Open the door,' they said, over and over. I told them to fuck off through the locked door a few more times. It felt good.

———

'Your father was fairly welcoming,' Miss Duffy said, and she sat heavily into a chair as if she was exhausted.

I said nothing. I suspected she was lying ... again.

'We went to visit your aunts,' Miss Thomas told me. 'Your father really is ... well ... I prayed all the way home for him, Anne Marie. I will pray again tonight. We all will.'

'Your aunts were quite forthcoming,' Miss Duffy said then, and Miss Thomas nodded, 'and they really understand your vocation.'

I hated the way I felt when she said that, imagining all of the big chat with my aunts about me and my parents. I felt completely powerless, and it felt disloyal to even hear it.

'We are your family now,' Miss Duffy said. 'Opus Dei is your mother and your father now. You mustn't worry; you don't ever have to go back.'

I shook my head. 'I ...'

But I didn't know what to say or how to say it.

'Let's pray,' the two women said, and they went to the oratory. So did I.

———

I don't remember turning 17, 18, 19 or 20, but I remember going between centres in Ireland, to do the same monotonous duties seven days a week, for years. Seven days a week, morning until night, silently cleaning for no pay, trafficked, enslaved and unhappy.

They moved me back to Lisdara again. Years were a blur. But as my mind matured, I started to find ways to think, usually while working, and I contemplated the life I was living very much, all the time.

I remember these double teak doors at the end of the corridor in Lisdara, orange tiles running up to it. The large steel gates were just outside of those doors, but nobody ever opened them. Everyone came in and out the other way. Doors and windows in Opus Dei buildings were always closed, even on the hottest days. I remember one day when I burned an egg in the kitchen and one of the others opened a window. The fresh air flew in upon us, lifting our hair off our necks and soothing our hot skin, and it felt like heaven. I remember pulling myself up to sit on the ledge beside the window, and closing my eyes and dreaming of freedom.

My imagination came back in dribs and drabs. Now in my early twenties, I imagined having a flat of my own. I thought about how I would paint it, and what kinds of decorations I would have. It would look nothing like this. I would have open windows and fresh flowers and paintings from abroad that I could buy when I travelled.

I would scrub the floors in Lisdara and sometimes sit back on my hunkers and look at those doors and imagine them opening up so I could run through them. I used to ask in my own head, *Have I done enough?*, as if it could ever be answered. I would ask it and listen, for the voice of God or whatever it was that other people could hear in there. But it never came.

Can I go now?

Nothing.

Would You forgive me if I left this life and went back?

Nothing.

Are You there at all?

Nothing.

Then Opus Dei moved me to a single room right beside those doors and I thought I was cracking up. It felt as though I was being taunted.

———

Miss Thomas and Miss Duffy told me that if I wanted to go home I would have to seek permission from Don Álvaro del Portillo. They were insistent on this. In order to go home I needed to be able to avoid temptation and continue with my full set of Norms. They felt I was not strong enough to avoid temptation and to continue with the Norms. I was not sure what they meant by temptation at home – was it the newspapers at home or was it stuff on the TV or the music on the radio? It was just called temptation, and apparently my family home was full of it. They had seen it themselves, they said. I could not get up and go home because I needed permission.

It was a mind game.

Later I would learn that this so-called permission was never actually required. The letter I wrote was likely never actually sent. It was another way of holding assistant numeraries there to work. It was a con. It was lies.

But I was a dog with a bone. I wrote the letter.

———

'Okay, Anne Marie,' Miss Duffy said. 'You got the permission from Rome' – she gave a subtle eye roll – 'but just for one overnight.'

My whole body felt light with the news. But I was scared too.

'We'll bring you and collect you,' Miss Thomas announced.

'Thank you,' I said. 'I'll come back,' I added in a rush, in case they'd change their minds. 'I will come back the next day.'

I felt like any minute they would take it back. So I just nodded and agreed and said thank you. I asked no questions, and gave vague answers.

'Opus Dei is your family,' Miss Thomas repeated, pressing the words into the air. 'You have a blood family, but you are committed to your Opus Dei family now. Remember that.'

It hurt me when they said things like that. I found it very unfair. My parents did go to Mass, sure so did everyone, but they were not more religious than that. My dad liked a pint, and loved the craic, played cards, and he smoked. There was tension at home sometimes between my parents. But the numeraries' commentary on what they thought went on at my home did not sit well with me. They made God feel like hate and fear and upset. But the God outside of Opus Dei seemed kinder. Just like my parents, my aunts, my friends, Niamh and her parents, the Murphys – they felt like warmth and like happiness.

'The Devil does that,' Miss O'Rourke had told me one time when I said why I missed my village. 'The Devil trains his servants so that they feel good to be around – it's a trick.'

It didn't feel like one, but she knew the truth of all of it.

They prepared me for days for the visit home. I was given the answers to every possible combination of questions.

'You love your life here,' Miss Duffy said, 'don't you?'

I said I did, and she made me repeat it: 'I love my life here, I have a vocation, I love Opus Dei, they are my family, this is my life mission, God has spoken to me and I know what I want to do with my life.'

'Your father is likely to cause you trouble,' she told me then.

I shook my head, but I didn't really know what she meant.

My dad was lovely; there was nothing troublesome about him.

'With coming back,' she went on. 'He will try to stop you, Anne Marie.'

I said I really didn't think so.

'Right so,' Miss Duffy said. 'Well, I think your father will still have to put a promise in writing that he will allow you to return to your home and vocation.'

Miss Thomas told me what to write to him and she posted it.

His response arrived a couple of days after.

Miss Thomas called me into her office and asked me to sit while she read out his letter to me. From her facial expression, she clearly felt she had outwitted my dad.

I never held his letter, but I could see it was perfectly written in his lovely handwriting. Things were happening fast and I had absolutely no control over any of them.

Twenty-eight

Before I could arrange to go home, I had to go to Confession to Father Thorton, the Opus Dei priest from Gort Ard. 'A clean soul to deal with the outside,' Miss Thomas said, as if the outside world was full of sins flying around waiting to stick to me like burrs.

The priest brought up the home visit as soon as I knelt down. He had been thoroughly briefed. 'Are you worried about your family?' he asked. 'I believe things are tough.'

'I'll just go for one night,' I said, terrified that the wrong line would get my visit privileges revoked.

'And your father, he won't try to stop you from returning?'

I shook my head.

'It is clear to me, Anne Marie,' he said, leaning forward, 'that you have a vocation to serve, and it is clear that to be an assistant numerary is your true calling. You must fight so hard for it, do you know?'

I did know, I said so.

'You must fight temptation at all times,' he said again. 'Now let us pray together for the strength you need.' He blessed the air in my direction, and lowered his head, and the two of us rambled off the words to the confessional prayers. The words were mumbo-jumbo – Latin – but I knew them off by heart. I just didn't know what they meant.

The directors prepared me for the trip. Miss Thomas held up a £50 note pinched between the fingers and thumbs of both hands as if it was the Host in Mass.

'You will take this money with you,' she said, holding it forward so I could take it. 'Keep it in your ... underwear.' A dirty word.

I took it and held it against my chest, flat under my palm, as they ran through the plan should my family protest my return.

'That money,' they said, 'will get you back to us.'

I was to run away at night-time, get a bus or train, ring them from a phone box, and they would come and collect me.

'And don't you forget to scream,' Miss Thomas said, 'as loud as you can, and run!'

———

Miss Thomas and her mother, Bridie, were the ones who drove me to Ballyvourney on the day. My dad wanted me to get the bus down but they said no, because that would be giving him control and me freedom. If they drove they could keep control.

'There is no need to explain our ways,' Miss Thomas said on the way. I was in the back of their two-door car. When we got in, both of them had locked their doors. There were no windows in the back, just these small panes that pushed open about an inch. On the long drive there we recited the 15 decades of the rosary and Bridie read from a book about the life of St Catherine of Siena, a Doctor of the Church. She was almost green with motion sickness trying to read it but she kept going to the end of the book.

Finally we arrived at the house. 'Stay in the car,' Breda said as she opened her door and put her feet out onto the ground. She twisted back to look at me. 'We will check and see what the situation is.'

I nodded, clinging onto each seat with my hands. In a moment my father came out, and he leaned in. 'Is it you, then?' he said.

I smiled a bit and nodded. He nodded behind him. 'Mam is here.'

I could see my mother, pale, standing at the door. She sidestepped to let the women pass into the house. My dad offered me a hand and I got out of the car. But then he didn't let go of it. He held it under his arm, and crossed his other hand to hold my wrist.

My stomach was churning with the plan. I would have to follow it, if he caused a fuss.

Scream and run.

We went into the house.

Scream and run.

Dad was saying to the women that I was staying home and not returning.

My mother asked them to leave.

Scream and – I opened my mouth and screamed.

The whole fill of my lungs poured out of me in a vibrating wail as my dad began pushing the two women toward the door. He flapped his arms and shouted at them to get out *now*.

They backed up.

Mam kept a hold of me.

'Anne Marie.' Miss Thomas put a hand out, and went in for a hug. 'Run away tonight,' she whispered quickly into my ear.

Mam held onto my hand, and her other hand grabbed my cardigan at my shoulder. 'Leave and do not come back,' she said to the numeraries.

I was still screaming but I didn't mean it. I didn't know how not to.

'Get out!' roared my dad again, suddenly twice his size, waving his arms up and down like a farmer to an advancing bull.

'Anne Marie,' my mother said, 'sit on that couch now!'

I sat down.

Maybe for effect, I screamed again, even though I didn't know why I was doing it. My vision blurred and my head felt like it was going to pop. Demons swooped for me, the air choked me. I felt like I was going to be sick.

The women gave up and left.

My father shut the door.

My mother sat on the couch and lit a cigarette. I could see her hands were shaking and she kept her eyes on my dad.

The car drove out the driveway.

The lid on Pandora's box finally closed and the place went quiet.

'Now,' Dad said, and he turned around, 'bring your bag to your room. Just know that you will never be going back there. Not over my dead body.'

He switched on the television and started to watch it, sitting in his chair and kicking his shoes off. He lit a cigarette and my mother pulled the curtains and sat down too.

The normality dazed me. I went to my room and started to pray like crazy.

———

My family watched me like hawks. I realised after a few days that any time I was down the stairs in our house, someone else was there. If it wasn't one of my parents it was a relation; if it wasn't a relation it was a friend or a neighbour. Everyone was in on this. But in a weird way, I was also in on it. They thought I might run, but I don't think I would have. But I was unsettled, I can tell you that.

I was caught between two worlds, the one I had always wanted – the real one – and the one I had been brainwashed into – Opus Dei. I bounced from one to the other, as I had done for the last five years, and it wasn't easy to understand myself. One minute I would be so relieved that I could sleep and eat and not be working all day every day, and feeling excited for a future in the normal world, and the next minute I would be absolutely terrified and trying to form an escape plan. I missed the monotony, in a weird way. I missed knowing what was happening. I was like an animal escaped from the zoo, galloping toward freedom but returning for feeding time.

If I made in any way toward the door, whoever was watching me would stand up, acting suspiciously casual, and say, 'Where are you going?'

It started to get on my nerves.

'To the phone box,' I said one day to my brother Eddie, who had been half asleep on the couch watching TV. The fire was dwindling a bit and he was just sitting up and reaching for the spade to shovel a bit of coal on, when I started putting my coat on.

'For what?' he demanded, dropping the shovel and standing up.

'A phone call,' I said, as if it was nothing.

I wanted to speak to them.

'To who?' he asked.

'A friend,' I said. I stared at him and he stared at me.

'You're not leaving the house, and sure you have no friends,' he said, jutting his chin out at me, 'You're not making a phone call. I'll get Dad if you so much as move.'

I knew I would have the call made before he would get to Dad, but I didn't want the drama, so I took my coat off and went back to my room.

'Can I use your phone?' I asked a shop attendant one day, when Mam and I were shopping in the local town. Mam was in the shop next door.

'Sure you can,' the woman said, but as soon as I lifted the receiver Mam came in and I put it back down.

'What are you doing?' she asked, frowning. 'Are you trying to call that crowd?'

I stood there, scared.

'Jesus,' Mam said. 'You are a nightmare.'

She bustled me out the door to the bus station.

'You are not to call those people,' she said, 'ever, ever again.'

'If I do not follow my vocation,' I said, 'we will all go to Hell.'

'Hell?' Mam's face went white, and we went home and she told my dad.

I was to be watched, he said, not let out of their sight. 'You've been brainwashed,' he told me.

So from then on, I had to go into work with my mother. I went every day with her after that.

'Work has always kept me going,' Mam said a few times a day. I knew that already.

Being out and about with my mother, in the real world, made me feel a million miles from Opus Dei and all the centres where I had worked so hard. My muscles, hard from scrubbing and cleaning all day, didn't hurt as much as time at home went on, and although at first I lost a bit of sleep to nightmares, gradually I started sleeping better, with the window open even on freezing nights.

One day in my mother's office the phone rang, and the receptionist answered it.

'She is here, yes,' she said, and handed me the phone. 'It's the Revenue Office looking for you.'

'The tax man?' I said, and put the receiver to my ear.

'Anne Marie, don't say one word,' a woman's voice said, low. I recognised it.

Miss Smith. My heart jumped into my throat.

'Anne Marie,' she said, 'your Opus Dei family have not given up. We are going to get you back, do not worry. Get the first bus you can get, and as soon as you can. We will meet you wherever it goes.'

I couldn't speak. I was filled with deafening confusion. Her voice frightened me – why was that? Hadn't I tried to phone her myself the week before?

'Anne Marie,' she continued, 'listen. You are in extreme moral danger, do you understand that? You are open to temptation and you must be strong. The Devil will put every temptation in your way.'

I nodded against the phone.

'Are you doing your Norms?' she asked.

'Yes.' My heart sped up.

'What will happen if you are living in sin?'

'I don't know what you mean,' I said.

'With a boy,' she said. 'Are you living in sin with a boy?'

'No,' I said, feeling thrown by the question. I thought it was a really weird thing to say.

'We will get you back, don't worry,' she said, and hung up the phone.

'So the tax man rang you? Do you think we are stupid?' my mother asked when I left the office. 'You don't even have an RSI number.'

I said nothing.

Twenty-nine

Opus Dei stalked me.

'They've called here twice looking for you,' my aunt Eileen told me down the phone. 'The first time I accidentally let them in, and to be honest they frightened the shite out of me, Anne Marie, I'll be honest now. I want you to stay away from those people.'

I was curious. 'What did they say?'

'That you had to follow your vocation,' she said, 'and they asked us to talk to you to go back or all of us would get sick or die and go to Hell.'

My mouth went dry. 'Who did you speak to?'

'That doesn't matter,' she said. 'You just make sure you stay away from them. They're mental.'

My dad was furious. 'They had absolutely no right to go near any family member,' he said. 'They've been up behind us as well, at Tom and Irene's place, making a nuisance.'

Tom and Irene were relatives of my fathers. They lived up the way and kept themselves to themselves, we really only saw them at Christmas.

The Opus Dei directors were outside my house another day. Two of them, Noreen Smith and a woman I had never met. I started walking backwards when I saw them; then they saw me and crossed the street to catch me, so I started to walk faster.

'We just want to talk!' Miss Smith shouted, raising her hand to wave me down as she crossed. She caught up with me, grabbing me by the shoulder and swinging me around. 'Are you all right?' she asked, leaning and looking into my face. 'Are you okay? Are they hurting you?'

My mind boggled. 'Nobody is hurting me,' I said. 'My family don't want me to talk to you.'

'We are your family,' the other woman said. 'Opus Dei are your family, Anne Marie – you made a commitment to Opus Dei.'

I kept going.

'Anne Marie!' Noreen Smith cried after me. 'You are losing your mortal soul to the Devil!!'

She wailed after she said it and as I looked over my shoulder I saw them staring. It spooked me. The dramatics of it all were so insincere.

A week later two women from Opus Dei called in to see my grandmother. She was 85 and lived alone. Then my dad's sister had taken a phone call from her, in a terrible state over what those women had said to her.

'They frightened her half to death!' said Dad. My mam was crying over it, sitting at the table.

'Unbelievable,' my dad said. 'They told her that she and all of us would burn in Hell. Do they really think we would send Anne Marie back now after that, do they?'

'Maybe I should go back,' I suggested, and I meant it, 'they might go to Nana's again.'

My dad said, 'Nana is under orders to not answer, and to call the Gardaí. Let's just hope they are stupid enough to call in to Paddy.'

Paddy was a relation who was a garda, and of course Opus Dei didn't realise. Of course they went there too.

'He ran them out,' Dad said, 'warned them not to go near us again or they'd be arrested.'

We all hoped that would be that.

———

I saw Miss Smith before she saw me. She was standing at the gates of my job, beside her car, looking around, but when I came around the corner she was looking up the other way. My first reaction was this creeping sense of guilt, like I had been caught with something dirty by a peer. I felt it to my toes. She hadn't seen me yet, so I turned and walked away, fast and in at the wall, until I got back home. I came in the door, closed it, and pressed my back against it.

'What's wrong with you?' Dad asked, standing in the kitchen. 'Some fella after you? No such luck, says you.'

I shook my head and took off my scarf.

'Are you not supposed to be working?' he said.

'No,' I said, 'I got my days wrong. I'm going to my room, I don't want to see anyone.'

I went up the stairs.

In my room I lay on my bed. I prayed so much that they would not call. They seemed to be everywhere I was. How were they doing it? I think – though I was so confused about things – I knew that I was better off at home, and I wanted to be at home. Well, maybe not so much at home as not in Opus Dei. Home was the best place to be away from that.

'Niamh Moore is here,' my dad said, poking his head around my door. 'Will I tell her you're busy?'

I sat up. 'Obviously I don't mean Niamh,' I said, and he opened the door then, letting Niamh under his arm into my room.

'I promise the loonies didn't send me,' she said, and waved a bag. 'I just called to see how you are.' Then she sat down and after a big sigh she said, 'I saw Miss Smith drive by me just now. Was she here?'

I shook my head. 'I saw her and came home.'

'They're not good people,' she said, taking bottles of Lucozade out of the bag and handing one to me. 'You are ... don't go back.'

I picked at a spot on the blanket where the wool was worn, and said nothing. She opened her drink and so did I. The taste of it was something so familiar that I had forgotten. I hadn't had Lucozade in years.

'We got nothing, Anne Marie,' she said. 'We worked for two years and got nothing. My diploma is worthless. I can't get a job. I had to go back to school.'

I took a slow breath in. 'Sorry it's not worth anything.'

'I'm sorry, you know,' Niamh said, 'that I ever got us involved with those nutters.'

I fished for the truth. 'Do you really think they're nutters?'

'They definitely are,' she said. 'Whack jobs. You're so much better than them. They don't even know you. They have used you.'

Maybe that was true, but even if it wasn't, I was glad to hear it.

Niamh stood up and said she had to go. 'I don't think you should ever go back,' she said again. 'You are much better than them.'

I wanted that to be true.

———

My GP sent an immediate referral to the hospital as soon as he saw the state of me. The complaints I had had in Opus Dei mostly resolved after being at home for a while, but my skin still flared up a good bit, and he thought it would be worth a specialist looking at it, to see what might be done to make it better.

I got the bus to Cork City.

Those waiting rooms are all the same, red-and-white tiles on the floor, green walls, the hospital smell. A brown desk with Perspex around it, little circles cut out so the receptionists can hear you and you them.

I went inside, took a ticket and sat down, and there was nothing in that situation that made me think for one second I was in any danger. I waited to be called for the doctor, minding my own business.

No sooner had I sat down in the main waiting room than I saw the doors open, and Miss Thomas walked through, and she sat down beside me. She was furious.

'Anne Marie,' she said, 'where have you been? We have not heard from you. Have you been doing your Norms? Who gave you permission to buy those clothes? What have you in your bag?'

I sat in shock, not answering at first.

'How did you know I was here?' I asked when I got my breath.

'We rang up and pretended to be you, of course,' she said.

Somehow we were standing up and I was trying to get away from her, lifting my hands into the air away from her clutches.

'Anne Marie, come with me.' She grabbed my arm and pulled me.

'I can't.' I tried to think. 'I can't go.

'Anne Marie,' she said, and pulled me further along. I clung onto the corner of the wall. 'Listen to me, you need to go to Confession, you are in the state of mortal sin.'

'I'm not,' I said, 'I'm not.'

'The Devil is tempting you,' she said. 'You need Confession. An Opus Dei priest is waiting in a church nearby, quickly. We have a car waiting outside to bring you there.'

I still clung onto the wall and started to raise my voice. Passers-by looked on and scurried past, afraid of the drama that was unfolding. I was afraid of it.

'People are looking at you,' she said.

'Don't touch me,' I said, barely able to catch my breath, 'don't touch me.'

We sat down, and she asked me if I was thinking of leaving Opus Dei, and for the first time in my life I whispered that I was. I did not look at her as I said it. She took out a pen and paper and told me to write to the Father and tell him I was thinking of leaving Opus Dei. I did what she instructed because I wanted to get away from her. She walked away and that was the last time I ever saw her.

———

Dad popped his head around the door.

'What are you doing?' he asked.

I didn't have an answer for him. Staring into space? I didn't know how to be at home, but I wanted to be. I wanted to be a normal Irish girl and just go to Mass on Sundays. I believed in God, and I knew He wouldn't want me to be so miserable. God wanted me to really live, to have fun and laugh. I wanted to be like the girls were around here, free to make mistakes, free to laze, free to talk and laugh and squeal if they wanted to. My heart said God wanted that too.

'A few of the lads are going into Kenmare later,' Dad said.

'Right,' I said.

He leaned against the door, drummed out a little beat on the wood. 'There's a band, uh … can't remember the name of them now but … they're all right.'

'Right,' I said. I wanted the conversation to go on. It felt like comfort, it felt real.

'Can't remember the name of them,' he repeated.

'Are they from Cork?' I asked, pretending to think.

'Not sure,' he said, 'but they're all right anyway, not terrible anyway.'

His face broke into a smile when he said that. He knew he was being shy.

'Right,' I said again.

'Maybe you'd have a think about going. It would be good for you,' he said.

'To see the band?' My hands went to the skin on my wrists and pinched, but I caught them in each other and held them.

Dad nodded. 'Sure why not?'

'Sure why not?' I repeated.

'What else have you to do?' he asked. 'You have this place spotless, like a hospital so it is.' He smiled at me.

I smiled back.

'You could do surgery in it,' he said.

I laughed out loud then.

'You'll go then?' he asked, checking.

'Sure why not,' I said again. 'I will.'

'What else have you to be doing?' he asked again as he turned away to go back downstairs. 'The place is like a lab.'

I put on my purple kilt and yellow shirt and looked in the mirror. My hands went up to my hair and I fixed it a bit, thinking about the style that was in, where you pushed it all over to one side to show your ear, letting it fall over your eye a bit. Did that suit me?

It felt really exciting to have plans to be going out. But I was also upset inside, battling against the fear Opus Dei had driven into me about these things. The fear of God and temptation everywhere.

Which was it? I thought. God, or eternal damnation? Which one was I afraid of? How could I be fearful of both? Was God sending me to Hell or was the Devil dragging me there? Could I trust neither?

I thought about Rose and her self-destruction. I thought about Niamh and her giggle and zest for living. Which of those two women did I want to be?

I knew. I knew.

I pushed my feet into my new shoes and looked down. My

toes didn't know themselves with all the room. Car headlights flashed through my closed curtain and I heard the sharp toot of a Citroën Dyane horn.

'You right?' Dad called, going down the stairs.

I took a deep breath and went out to the car that had pulled up, cramming in beside people whom I had last seen as teenagers, now adults.

The passenger in the front turned and looked at me. 'Jaysus, Anne Marie, are you coming out?'

I knew him, it was Diarmuid from my class. He had grown into himself over the years.

I nodded and he shot me a smile. 'Brilliant,' he said. 'I'll have to get a first round in to celebrate you coming home.'

'You will,' I said, feeling brave.

In the pub he bought us all a drink. I took a breath and asked for a glass of lager and lime. I'd have one. I could say a prayer later, just in case, but right now I needed to do this for myself.

The few of us that were there got straight into conversations, about the Dunlop factory closing and unemployment, and then about women's rights in Ireland. I had strong opinions, and I gushed to express them. All the thoughts I had under the surface.

'I'm caged enough as a woman,' I said, 'caged by culture, but I don't know if I think women should be caged by marriage. We should be free to leave a bad marriage.' The words I said, the beliefs I had, went totally against Opus Dei, and there were small flinches when I felt the fear of their brainwashed beliefs, but I wanted my bravery – these were my thoughts, not theirs.

Diarmuid sidled up and clinked his glass against mine. 'So, what are you up to?'

'Not much, working with my mam in the factory,' I said. 'Keeps me busy.'

'Right,' he said. 'Have you spare time?'

'Not really,' I said, even though I did. Keeping our house was like a holiday in comparison to the work I had been doing for Opus Dei.

'Do you dance?' he asked, one hand in his pocket, lifting his glass toward the dancefloor.

'No,' I said firmly, 'I don't.'

He nodded and took a drink from his pint.

I looked at the people on the dancefloor and thought about what I had just said. If I was Anne Marie Allen from Ballyvourney, then that was a lie. She danced all the time, any chance she got. If I was Anne Marie from Opus Dei, it was the truth, I supposed, because we never danced or listened to music or had fun.

Who am I?

I had no idea. Someone in the middle of those two people, perhaps. A better version? I didn't think so; not better. I was in between.

'I don't know the new dances,' I said then.

He finished his drink in one go.

'Me neither, to be honest,' he said. I could smell the washing powder from his shirt. It was rolled up at the sleeves, and open at the neck. He was handsome.

'Me neither,' I said back again, and then we both burst out laughing.

'Will we give it a shot?' he asked, nodding his head toward the floor.

'I don't know this one though,' I said. 'Maybe in a while.'

'Nah,' he said grabbing my hand, 'I'm not putting up with that – let's go.'

He twirled me under his arm, and then we were in the throng of dancing people, shuffling back and forward trying to get the hang of it all.

I told myself I could be there. I told myself it was okay. This was my life, *my* beautiful life. I only had one.

I didn't have to punish myself for living.

I didn't have to get onto my hands and knees and beg for forgiveness for my humanity.

Surely.

The girl next to me had the steps right; I could see that from how smoothly she rolled from one foot to the other, swishing her hips in the opposite direction and raising her hands, elbows crooked, above her head. I copied her, and it worked for me. It had been so long since I'd danced, but it was easy for me, it seemed, to do again.

Diarmuid leaned in to speak into my ear. 'I thought you said you didn't know how to dance.'

'I forgot how,' I said, 'but I remember now, I remember now!'

The music caught me at the same time as his hand caught mine, twirling me out into another space, a bigger one, where I wasn't as sure of myself, but where I was so, so happy and so, so free.

'Go, Anne Marie, go!' I opened my eyes to see the rest join us. Strangers caught my eye and smiled at me, and I smiled at them.

It felt wonderful. The music took me over and I closed my eyes and let my body follow the beat. It didn't matter if I wasn't perfect, it really didn't matter.

I twirled and twirled and smiled and smiled.

This was where I'd stay. This was me. *This* was what I was built for.

Epilogue

I officially left Opus Dei on 19 March 1985. At first I struggled hugely but eventually I got my Leaving Cert and went to college. Then I started work with the Prison Service, where I had a wonderful career for 30 years. I remember that what struck me so strongly with prisoners was how much they needed changes in routine and interests and things to keep them going. I put a lot of work into ensuring these options were available, filling their spaces with books and music and making sure they could opt in to education and live as well as they could in confinement. I always focused on the human rights of everyone I came across, for both staff and prisoners. I hope it made a difference.

As I went through the process of writing this book, I was forced to think deeply about my past, but also about where I am now in my life. I looked around so many times and looked at my lovely little house and my wonderful son and I thought about how lucky I am to have gotten away from Opus Dei.

Now retired, I give my time to executive coaching. I understand what feeling lost is; my own life journey has been filled with doubt – and it still is – but reclaiming my voice is part of what fuels my work. Now I walk beside others as they rebuild their self-trust; I use my scars to light their way, and every breakthrough with them heals a part of me.

I often lie awake and think about the assistant numeraries who haven't left. The ones who live in the basements and corridors of those big houses. In the mornings, right when I open my eyes, I think about the girls scrubbing and hoovering and cooking all day long with no break, never getting a day to lie in bed. I pull my covers up and lie in and feel so glad of it.

Then I think about the women being manipulated to join right now, and I know they are why I am speaking out. They are why I have to. I didn't always think that, and it was a long road to get to a place where I feel brave. To say the words 'I was in a cult' is still scary to me, because their threats sit inside my brain even now, and I still feel the same fear. But I do it anyway – isn't that the advice? It's okay that I am scared, but I need to speak out.

I was a child when Opus Dei groomed me into their organisation. I was a child when I took vows in Rome without the knowledge of my parents. I was a child when I was put to work, trafficked between institutions, and I was a child when I was encouraged – and at times strong-armed – to commit self-harm. Those things have affected my entire life since.

For most of my life, I kept my experiences to myself. I went to college, got a degree, and I went to work in the Prison Service – and had a long, happy career there. If I could put it simply, I stayed silent. Silent because they told me to: *Say nothing, or we will come after you. Bad things will happen to you, to yours.* I obeyed, even as their words carved scars into my life. Even as I suffocated under the weight of what they did to me. So why speak now? I speak because I owe the world the truth about their abuse. I speak to stop them from stealing more lives. I speak for the thousands like me, still trapped in Opus Dei's shadows, still aching for justice.

For years, I blamed myself. How could I have been so naïve? So weak? But the shame has faded now. I see clearly: I was young, vulnerable, hungry for purpose – a perfect target. They came armed with their rules, their saints, their lies, and I stood no chance. Their grooming was a trap, and I was ripe for the picking.

I am not ashamed any more. I am angry. Justifiably, unapologetically angry. Angry that Opus Dei exists – a relic of cruelty with no place in this world. Angry that they hunt children, plucking them from poverty and innocence to fill their ranks. Angry that their Founder – a canonised saint – built his empire on the backs of girls like me, threatening hellfire if we refused to serve their elite. Angry that the Church blessed this corruption. Angry that they erased us, scrubbing our names from memory the moment we fled. Angry that they still lie, still defend him, still steal lives like thieves in the night.

Opus Dei took so much from me. But here's what they can never take: my rage. My grief. My refusal to let them define me forever. What saved me? Life. Life in its messy, glorious noise: music blaring (the good, the bad, the gloriously mediocre!), my son's laughter echoing through our home, friendships that feel like sunlight, and the sacred act of cooking feasts for those I love. Learning, always learning – politics, cultures, the thrill of fresh air biting my cheeks as I walk. Travelling the world in shoes I choose myself – no dogma, no rules, just colour. The radio humming each morning, playing whatever I damn well please. Healing brick by brick, until the girl they buried began to breathe again.

Healing? It's slow. Maybe I will never fully heal; I ignored the wound for so long. But I look around my home, filled with trinkets and photographs and books, and I know I am doing well. I don't consider God to notice or care. I wear bright colours. I laugh my head off. I choose what I eat, what I read, who I am. And I speak, because if I don't, they'll keep devouring others.

Opus Dei did give me one wonderful, wonderful gift, however. What was it? Finding *us*. The ones who escaped. I thought I was alone – how wrong I was. Eileen, Teena, Deirdre, Claudine, Margaret, Sheila, Tita … Women once labelled 'servant' now roaring with life, laughter, defiance. Together, we are stronger. Across continents – Argentina, Mexico, Spain – we gather on Zooms, on forums, in whispered confessions. We share stories like lifelines, stitching our broken pieces into something whole. I have met many hundreds of other ex-members, both male and female, through www.opuslibros.org and on forums. So many like me are starting to tell their stories, exposing the truth behind the closed doors.

Opus Dei wanted us afraid. Now? We want *them* afraid – of the stories we'll tell, the justice we'll demand, the lives we'll rebuild without their permission. I want their palaces to crumble and the people they destroyed, rebuilt.

I go back sometimes to Ballyglunin House. It's under new ownership, and its walls are filled once again with human art, love and laughter. The first time I went back wasn't easy. The ghosts still linger.

People ask me why I go back there, why there specifically. And the truth is I'm not sure why. I think I go there to reach out to the kid I was before all of this – that little anxious, dancing girl. I can never have her back; that's the sad thing. I can't rush through time and grab her up and tell her, 'You matter.' It's clear to me now that was what Opus Dei used to trap me: how little I thought of myself, how much I needed encouragement and praise to feel like I had a place on this earth – they used that. They tricked me.

Maybe I go back to Ballyglunin because each time I do, I leave again. The strength comes to me each time I open that door and walk down that path and out the forbidden gate – and I am a free woman. Because every time I do, some little missing part of the child that is still trapped there clutches on as I pass by, down the hall and out the door, and is freed too. With every step, she is reclaimed. Each time I go back, it's like I recover a little part of me again, piece by piece, and I leave taller, fiercer, more my *own* than before.

Acknowledgements

To those whose actions brought darkness into my life through the oppressive control of Opus Dei, I hope this serves as a reflection of the harm inflicted. Your teachings brought me nothing but falsehoods – telling me I would be unhappy, useless and unwanted outside your realm. You painted the world beyond Opus Dei as unforgiving, but you were wrong. After leaving Opus Dei the world welcomed me with warmth and kindness.

To the people of Ballyvourney, I cannot express enough gratitude for the compassion and caring you showed me. In those crucial days, weeks and months after I left, you embraced me without hesitation, offering encouragement and guidance that I will never forget.

I am incredibly grateful to those who believed in me, even when some didn't know my full story. Your faith empowered me to grow and reach heights I never thought I would, and I am forever thankful.

A special thanks goes to my solicitor, Dominic Creedon, for standing by me in my pursuit of justice from the beginning. To *Financial Times* journalist Antonia Cundy, for her belief in my story and her dedication to exposing human rights violations, thank you. To my many friends and extended family, your loyalty, through thick and thin, has been my anchor.

To the Ballyglunin community and the current owners of Ballyglunin Park, thank you for your support and for helping me heal.

To Argentinian lawyer Sebastian Sal and the 43 former assistant numeraries, thank you for your extraordinary bravery in the pursuit of justice. I'm honoured to stand with ex-Opus Dei numerary Eileen Johnson, who has fought tirelessly for truth and accountability for decades. My heartfelt thanks extend to ex-Irish assistant numeraries Teena, Maureen, Sheila, Claudine, Deirdre, and all ex-members of Opus Dei who are committed to exposing the truth. Together, we will continue to shine a light on the exploitation of children, human trafficking and human rights abuses perpetrated by Opus Dei.

I am deeply grateful to Liosa McNamara for her unwavering patience, compassionate understanding, and for always listening with such care and kindness throughout the journey of writing this book together.

To my brother Johnny, thank you for steadfastly standing by me since 1983. To Paul, your unwavering support has been incredible. And to my amazing son, Matthew, your extraordinary bravery and unfaltering strength inspires me every single day.